THE POWER
Part 1
Sonia Gandhi

Roopa Venktesh

Paperback: 978-1-967820-12-2
eBook: 978-1-967820-11-5
Library of Congress Control Number: 2025908235

This is a work of nonfiction.

Ordering Information:

Prime Seven Media
518 Landmann St.
Tomah City, WI 54660

Printed in the United States of America

Secondary ordering of the books may also be exclusively obtained by the author

Contact information -Dr Roopa Venktesh Hongirana No 48 Bar One
4 th A cross Pipeline road Vijaynagar Bangalore 560040
Karnataka India

Address in the UK -Number 6 Penwell Fold Oldham OL1 2UB
United Kingdom

Sonia Gandhi shows heartfelt happiness while addressing her Congress party supporters. She is happy amongst her happy Congress supporters. This is the reason she never wishes to stop working hard for her people Sonia Gandhi addressing AICC members at Talkatora Stadium, New Delhi on Nov 2 2010

TABLE OF CONTENTS

INTRODUCTION

I have written this book in good faith, entirely and purely with the hope that it will be a source of inspiration to perhaps every woman – mother, daughter, sister – no matter what her life's endeavour. We are all multitaskers of sorts. Every woman should perhaps dare to dream. Sonia Gandhi has been a great influence to a commoner like myself. It is not my intention by any means to belittle the thoughts of those who might wish to disagree with the ideas and thoughts I present in this book. My earnest thought is that no one should oppose the ideals of Sonia Gandhi in keeping with harmony, peace, and tolerance in every society.

Any constructive feedback may be e-mailed to me at roopavenktesh@gmail.com, roopavenktesh@yahoo.co.uk, and roopabedigere7@gmail.com I will make an attempt to incorporate responses in future books in this series. All Correspondences from persons who do not identify themselves shall not receive a response. Readers may appreciate that this book, as part one of the series, may appear incomplete in many respects; The good intent is to clear the misconceptions of many critics, so very few have been touched upon in this book.

All material has been properly referenced, a large part of the matter presented in this book from credible public sources as appropriate. Also accessed are some lesser known resources..Because this book has been self published for constructive, informal use, I ask that anyone who contests any of the content simply contact me. Any use of this material to promote controversy is strictly prohibited and shall never be entertained ever. I,Dr Roopa Venktesh hereby declare I take no responsibility, legal or otherwise, for any omission or misrepresentation implicit or explicit, any controversy implicit or explicit, intended or unintended, as it shall then defy my very basis for writing this book, which is nothing but good faith. I hereby solemnly declare that I have not been contacted by any official sources related to the Indian National Congress party. Under no account do I express implicit or explicit bias in terms of race, religion, nationality, culture, or other variable. No funds have been derived from any party in India, especially the Congress party, which in fact, was clear not to endorse my book. I endeavoured to go ahead with this book despite the fact that no political member from Congress came forth to endorse my book. I write purely to spread a strong timeless message of peace,harmony, tolerance, and freedom, and to inform readers about the many laudable steady principles that Sonia Gandhi has stood for by her unfailing work in the Congress party for a significant period of decades in a country that is not her birth country, is outside her comfort zone, and offers her continuing opposition. In health and sickness she perseveres

All the funds to make this self-published book are in fact entirely derived from my legitimate income, which I have earned working hard in my profession as a doctor in the United Kingdom. As a mother, I have struggled to establish my career, which posed many challenges because of discrimination against me based on my gender.

I present this book to my readers with the hope of rejuvenating the fundamentally human moral principles that should endure:

harmony, peace, and freedom,unity based on non-discrimination of gender, nationality, race, religion, language, and all other such variables. The list of such variables seems endless.

This book is to remind the Congress of the faith displayed by the respectful Sonia Gandhi when she renounced the coveted prime minister's office in 2004, and the faith that sustained the Congress in remarkable, successful Congress-led initiatives under her leadership (and other varied dynamic roles such as the UPA chair till date)

I found a classic role model in Sonia Gandhi when I faced a rough patch in my career. This book will pay a befitting tribute to Sonia Gandhi's principles of nonviolence and non-discrimination amongst many others. I can confirm that, when and if the respectful President Gandhi reads this book, she will be reading it at the same time all other readers read it. This is to only reaffirm that Sonia Gandhi has not endorsed this book.

My decision to write and release this book has been a long story fraught with time constraints as well as a lack of resources of all kinds. It has been a one- woman venture for me as an author. With a lack of endorsement, it was not easy to see my dream come true and see this book published. First few published editions of the same book did not sell and I lost further finances and yet with my perseverance my book Sonia Gandhi The Power Part 1 won an award. 'Book excellence award' for book design, content and market appeal. This application was sponsored by my classmate Dr Prathiha Venkatswamy MD California (My special thanks to her) https://bookexcellence.com/ project/2017-book-excellence- award-competition-results/

I wish to mention to all readers that this book has been self published The fact is I am in debts due to my investment for the book self-publication,republishing, self-funded Logan Crawford interview 2024 and now again republishing)

https://www.youtube.com/watch?v=roJXrQ2yEPs, critical reviews to this book also are entirely self-invested
https://www.blueinkreview.com/book-reviews/sonia-gandhi-part-1/
I have followed up data in the public domain ever since I met Soniaji in 2015 for a record 10 years till date I have come to understand the person I have conceived with compassion,care and respect to her and her unbeatable record of any single politician in a democracy for decades in an adopted country which now is her home is indeed a good overview of her career nonstop in politics from 1997 till date She serves as a member of Rajyasabha since Feb 20 2025 at the time of writing The failure of Congress in the 2014 elections in India made me be hopeful for Sonia Gandhi simply because of her undying devotion to the universal principles of peace, tolerance, and harmony. Despite my plan to release this as soon as possible, the work took a long time, and I am certain the timeless principles of peace, harmony, unity, and tolerance shall never fade. I sincerely hope that my book rejuvenates respect for these virtues for Sonia Gandhi(and any other leader or person of similar standing), which was perhaps forgotten in the 2014 elections(and all successive elections till date) by the Indian electorate. This book also urges readers to welcome tolerance and unity rather than fragmenting and fighting on the basis of endless variables like gender, race, nationality, and religion. Never before has the need for these principles arisen more powerfully than now in the ever- fighting and ever-disturbed world we live in as it happens.

I have not, in the process of applauding Sonia Gandhi, tried to contradict or undermine the ability of any other leader of political or non-political standing(including other members of her own family within and outside of the family). I can confirm without hesitation my unflinching support for Sonia Gandhi's principles of nonviolence, unity, tolerance, freedom, and non-discrimination of any possible kind. I have made an earnest attempt to focus on Sonia Gandhi, as I find her a living example of a person who has practised what she has tried to preach. All material is sourced from public domain only. Any inadvertent error or inaccuracy is neither my responsibility nor the responsibility of the publisher, as the idea of publishing this is just merely an exercise to create a book that is a 'good read' with a good strong take-away message of peace, harmony, and tolerance, and many other democratic ideals of the Congress party that appealed personally to me. It would be interesting to see an AI version of this book in future series

I self published, self funded interviews, self funded critical reviews https://www.blueinkreview.com/book-reviews/sonia-gandhi-part-1/

and hope to gain a natural audience under no coercion or influence. yet I sponsored facebook pages Ireland which had a stunning 50,000 responses from Non resident Indians who unanimously agreed to what I presented way back in 2015

I welcome traditional publishers to welcome content from self published work like this one from across the world This book was exhibited in five countries international book fairs (sponsored) and was exhibited in Frank Furt Book Fair Art Buchamese 2024 I also welcome Hollywood and other entertainment industry welcome inspiring content like this one so more impact can result out of the compelling narrative of this book content

I write this book with the plead that hopefully can encompass social media, inspire artists and educationists as a material to reflect upon or adapt

My hope for the current and future generations is that this work be translated to all languages of the world possible to inspire current and future leaders learn from nonviolent nonconfrontational strategic restraint, patience and peaceful nonwar measures to prosper in the world This is especially relevant to my fellow beings Israelis, Russians, Ukrainians, Palestinians and the volatile middle eastern nations (Iran and Syria being new entrants!)

At the time of updating this book, the author appreciates the stand of the respectful President Donald J Trump, United States 2025 making efforts to negotiate, pause and reopen strategies to secure communication

While I conducted my research, my understanding of this inspiring leader in Sonia was just so sentimental that I felt I should be able to communicate the appreciable decisions that Sonia Gandhi has made along her powerfully resilient political career. Her decisions have influenced society at large, Indian politics, and perhaps even politics in other parts of the globe as well. I know they influenced me – a struggling Indian woman mother – and helped me to set a sustained and enduring goal for success in both my personal and professional lives. I'm sure she (any leader who can emulate similar personal attributes of patience, perseverance and dynamism) can be an inspiration for others like me.

Sustained and enduring professional goals contribute to both personal and professional life because one influences the other so easily. Sonia Gandhi's management of both her professional and private life is exemplary.

At the time I was first inspired – a long time ago in the late nineties – Sonia Gandhi was not yet active politically. She remained in the background, conspicuously hushed behind the front lines of the Gandhi dynasty who held the power in Indian politics.

The images that I cannot erase from my mind are newspaper photographs reflecting the tragic assassinations of two family members utterly dear to Sonia Gandhi – her dear mother-in-law, Prime Minister Indira Gandhi, in 1984, and her dear spouse, Mr

Rajiv Gandhi, while he was campaigning, in 1991.Not to exclude the death of brother in law SanjayGandhi The images show Sonia Gandhi silently suffering yet speechless. It must have been difficult for her, facing a daunting future. This is the pre-mobile era pre-social media era every reader must appreciate

The Indian (electorate)public just poured such sympathy in the following elections that the majority simply voted for the Congress to empathize with the private lives of the Gandhi household following the assassination of Mr Rajiv Gandhi. These sacrifices are perhaps now long forgotten …These times politics happening in the rest of the world were not much known worldwide due to lack of the current times of globalization, social media and sponsored media

This book hopes to rejuvenate the thoughts of respect for such leaders in the Congress party. Aside from all the criticisms that Congress could do better, the power of the Gandhi dynasty can never be underestimated.

As I closely followed Sonia Gandhi's journey of motherhood alone as she cared for the future political promises, her son, Rahul, and her daughter, Priyanka, I could not but empathize with the way this resolute lady took the helm of the political affairs in India by accepting the position of Congress party president. The promises Sonia nurtured clearly are bright and undisputable in Priyanka Gandhi and Rahul Gandhi who hold the flagship firm Both Rahul and Priyanka are each an individual force and dual force and a threesome power together with Sonia Gandhi in all in various political visible moments something not easily seen in other parts of the world

It is all the more remarkable to me as a commoner who has struggled in the role of working mum. I have barely been able to fulfil the duties of a family typical in an Indian household under common, ordinary conditions and able to imagine the demands of decision making and patience. It must never be forgotten that Sonia Gandhi had all the liberty to choose not to work for the Congress, and I think she deserves great respect. Additionally, her decision to help Congress is praiseworthy particularly because the Congress party at that time was in much need of her leadership so it was not all a carpeted rosy dream. Sonia Gandhi not only accepted the presidency of the Congress, but nurtured the Congress rather strongly for decades to come. Despite all the unnecessary and harsh controversy surrounding her political life, this book pays tribute to Sonia Gandhi's remarkable and commendable journey into Indian politics, which is perhaps also relevant to politics anywhere else in the world. Having read all credible references, I find that the controversies around Sonia Gandhi mostly restrict themselves to the few incorrect references. In reality, there seems to be no substantial basis to the needless controversies raked in time and time again. I have deliberately omitted such needless controversies; for example, the widely publicized Bofors issue. My views on Sonia Gandhi in this book perhaps have the potential to gain importance because they represent the commoner's view of Sonia. This is why the views of the emerging global citizens are of increasing importance.I noted that most of the books about her or that refer to her, mostly lack a prophecy with regard to her plans or decisions for the political future of Indian politics. In my humble opinion the true best is yet to emerge maybe I have touched upon a few and far in between I hope to explore these in my future editions

The books I made references about were mostly authored by high profile personalities, and therefore my decision to continue to write this book was further encouraged, as it would perhaps emerge as a view of Sonia Gandhi in a larger perspective.

The special personal and professional attributes that have proven to be Sonia Gandhi's assets in her political journey, both actively and passively, are what I wish to highlight, along with her many other desirable political and personal attributes

Since I began my research in 2013, I have learnt about the journey of this powerful woman, Sonia Gandhi. I have been inspired to write about this enigmatic woman who has witnessed three generations of political journeys under one roof, so to speak, in the single household of the prestigious Gandhi-Nehru family.

I have often wondered and tried to understand how, as a reluctant politician, Sonia Gandhi not only holds the key in Indian politics but also knows to play it safe. She is cautionary yet political, anticipatory yet dramatic, challenging yet successful, unsuccessful yet only to spring back successfully.

Sonia Gandhi's role as president of Congress succeeded for an unprecedented consecutive decade and a half. In 2014 the world witnessed the largest democratic electorate vote, with Congress being the traditionally known and previously reasonably successful dynastic political party in India. Congress failed to impress the electorate as the traditional Congress did not exploit emerging patterns of media, social media and media technology Successively media especially sponsored media change patterns are perhaps affecting politics

Merely sustaining the power is itself a great job, let alone spearheading it to victory. Sonia Gandhi's prowess has been evident, as she is the longest-serving president of the Congress party, a party that perhaps would have found it difficult to survive on its own.

It is always a lot easier to criticize without basis or facts, and as Sonia Gandhi leads an intensely private life despite her role and work as a politician, it has been quite a task to understand the nuances of her laudable political decision making.

I rely on the outcome of her decisions, both political and private, which I feel are well deserved in order to appreciate all the fabulous political skills Sonia Gandhi has wielded in her political career.

My aim in writing this book is purely to showcase the attributes of Sonia Gandhi that have particularly made her name synonymous with power in global politics. With India's rapid and significant presence in the economic front nationally and internationally, the one woman certainly praiseworthy is perhaps India's answer to Thatcher of Britain.

I would imagine the success of *Sonia Gandhi: The Power* for me would be that her worshipful Sonia Gandhi sincerely liked the book. I also hope that my readers, as I have done, will find a lot of qualities in Sonia Gandhi to emulate – not just as a woman, but as a multitasker and a woman politician, and also as a mother and a complete family person in so many respects.

There have been more than forty books written in dedication to Sonia Gandhi. This is limited to my references from those catalogued in the British Library, London. Many of the authors, including Sonia Gandhi herself, who has authored several books, have perhaps presented the facts on matters relating to the astute politician as they have been eye witness. There are a lot of books dedicated to Sonia Gandhi exclusive of this list(stocked in The British Library) that have been published and sold in India and Asia alone. As I searched through the material, what was strikingly obvious was that there really was not much information about Sonia Gandhi, and that perhaps demonstrates that Sonia Gandhi is more of a politician with executive power than oratorical power. This executive power is singularly decisive; the steel of it lies in the power of Sonia Gandhi's style of functioning. The critics may say she is too powerful, but in my view this power is what holds the roots of the Congress firmly.

The books written about Sonia Gandhi speak more of anecdotes involving Sonia rather than Sonia herself. This also reflects the huge potential of many attributes unpublicized in Sonia Gandhi as a politician. Knowing well the power of the Gandhi household in Indian politics, I think it is phenomenal that Sonia Gandhi has put in practice the valuable experience she gained while she was a close witness to the powerful political roles her mother-in-law and her husband displayed during their respective tenures in the office of prime minister.

Sonia Gandhi shared a trusting, long-lasting relationship with both her mother-in-law and her husband. Despite apparent differences in nationality, race, religion, language, and so forth, their everlasting loving relationships remained intact, and it is fair to say the Indian people appreciate this till today. It is clear that this trust served her well even after her dear husband was no more. If anything, Sonia Gandhi's life appeared to be enlivened by the memories of the ever- charming Rajiv Gandhi as she dedicated her life to Congress whilst also encouraging her two children onto the same path.

A large part of the information presented in this book has been sourced from all the information presented in the public domain. Perhaps this book shall be very unique, as I have tried to present the information entirely from a global citizen point of view and have simply tried to establish what, why, where, when, and who, relating to the politics and success of Sonia Gandhi. It is my best intention to present what I think has been appealing in her as a wife, a mother, a politician, a multitasker, manager, and a silently successful person.

I sincerely hope my readers will understand and respect this excellent personality of Sonia Gandhi much as we respect many other global personalities. When such an intention is served, I shall understand that due credit will have been given for my efforts to write this book and accomplish my purpose. I hope my efforts and purpose will be taken in the spirit with which I have done my work, and I hope my readers will understand and respect the many ideals of Sonia Gandhi.

Dear readers, I welcome you to roll up your sleeves and read about the incredible life of Sonia Gandhi, who has had perhaps the strongest and most intrepid career in politics in recent decades on the planet in the world's largest democracy, India. Talking about democracy I hope the rest of the world embraces democracy as much as it can especially the war prone Russia, Israel, China, et al

Priyanka Gandhi Vadra is a bright political promise -- beauty, charm, legacy, and power all in one click. This promise is again nurtured by the Congress president and mother, her kindness Sonia Gandhi

Priyanka Gandhi is a born leader If I may view her as. She is born into a political family with all universal ingredients necessary for some significant politics that she effortlessly plays into Indian politics Priyanka Gandhi is a beautiful soft spoken and an intelligent leader who follows the successful political roles as a politician family be it the role of a ordinary party supporter, star campaigner,general secretary and leads into being super successful leader as a Member of Lok Sabha. She can lead politics anywhere across India, be it North or South, east or west of India. About Congress supporters outside of India Priyanka, a typical family Indian politician, is buttressed by brother Rahul who covers Indian interest in the Indian diaspora. She woos public by her charming presence everywhere possible, She is a politician with the self awareness and self consciousness of a true lead in public campaigns with her honest views to the press and public alike One moment we could see her supporting her mother's statements ,in yet another she could contest in her brothers constituency in another she could propel a Congress party loyalist into a winner She is clearly the politician of great intelligence,aura and focus She leaves no moment to stop acknowledgement of the Indian electorate and their pressing issues of national and international importance She is stepping her family's legacy forward with that much needed momentum, And as for campaigning or press,she is easily the media's tempting attention with her beautiful Indian attires and persona, she leaves no moment to impress every member of the public. She is sure to acknowledge thousands on a mass campaign as best as a single small child dying to catch her parents' attention. She is that political magic every leader could be envious of. Priyanka Gandhi is a slight contrast to mother Sonia Gandhi in her treatment of the press. Priyanka seizes every moment in press to market Congress' position more than ably and perhaps influences the media the way she would expect the public would have liked It is a skill in her that surpasses that of the media! She is clearly not in a race for the chair and in fact proposed a non Gandhi member to occupy the current presidency of the Indian National Congress

This leader is an all in one star of the Congress which holds a powerful and a shining promise as a political leader to watch She is a great speaker fluent in Hindi and English alike and appears to supplement but in a strict sense leads not the only the Congress but the national electorate as well in wielding a great influence on masses and media alike

The other noteworthy part is Sonia Gandhi Rahul gandhi and Priyanka Gandhi are a trio with a single goal of leading the Indian National Congress (INC).There is no dispute or disagreement in this fact as they portray different roles into the branches of INC each in no race for a single position or power. They have the inherent power of undisputable power well empowering the candidates to hold charge of.

Rahul Gandhi's achievements are not to be underestimated here (Though succeeds as a president of INC is as dynamic as mother Sonia and sister Priyanka) and I have tried to focus on the women politicians moreso on Sonia Gandhi

DEDICATION

The lotus feet of Lord Venkateshwara, Thirupati our family deity whose grace is memorable to me and the Lotus feet of the Supreme Lord Shri Krishna,Goddess Lakshmi and Goddess Saraswathi My family (Vaasudaiva Kutumbakam in Sanskrit means the world is a family), A G K Venkatesh, son Skanda Venkatesh, son Chandravarna Venkatesh, daughter Krishna Venkatesh my late parents Smt Kamala and Shri B A Shivaramaiah, brother Prakash Bedigere, sister Priya Gowda, My in laws Late Shri A G Krishnappa, Late Smt Kabbar Lakshmamma, my respectful Late grandfather Shri B N AppeGowda former Chairman, late grandfather Shri M S ShivananjeGowda, my late grandmother Smt Puttamma, last but not the least all the respectful well-wishers, curious readers and critics

ACKNOWLEDGEMENTS

The New Cambridge English School 1980-1990 Bangalore

MES COLLEGE of Arts Science and College 1990 –1992 Bangalore

Class of Bangalore Medical College Bangalore 1992 1992 Special mention' Subbu', Madhu of class BMC 92

SONIA GANDHI

It gives me immense pleasure to write about the respectful Sonia Gandhi, the president of the Indian National Congress, one of the major political parties of historic importance in India and, in fact, the political party which is of paramount importance despite a significant failure in the recent elections in 2014.

Sonia Gandhi is popularly known as Sonia or Soniaji in India, or simply Sonia Gandhi. In this book I refer to her as Sonia Gandhi everywhere (to avoid confusion with other women called Mrs Gandhi, like Mrs Indira Gandhi, Mrs Maneka Gandhi, and so forth). Sonia Gandhi's dear husband, the late Prime Minister Rajiv Gandhi, is said to have addressed Sonia Gandhi as *Son*, the Hindi word that means 'akin to gold'. In Russian, I have come to understand from my research, *sonia* means 'wisdom'.

I am somewhat embarrassed to introduce myself in front of the towering personality of Sonia Gandhi. However, I do wish my skeptical readers to know my background – what I did and why I wished to do so. Readers may then appreciate my attempt and intention of dedicating this book to Sonia Gandhi. While dedicating this book to Sonia Gandhi's struggle to uphold the values of unity, tolerance, peace, harmony and freedom, I wish to affirm that I stand by the same values. Perhaps Sonia Gandhi is the most misunderstood person today, and I sincerely hope that my book can change that perception.

I am an ordinary woman hailing from Bangalore in India. I am a professional doctor. I emigrated to England to pursue postgraduate training in general practice. This is called community medicine in many countries; family practice is another analogous term. I have no direct connection with politics or politicians, although as an Author my curiosity about the accomplishments of Sonia Gandhi could never be satisfied. I have developed the better part of my portfolio of writing for a largely philanthropic purpose. I wrote my first book as a DIY (do-it-yourself) guide, and I chose to write this book to help us reminisce about the strong ideals Sonia Gandhi has stood for, in particular a woman having to live in a adopting country.

I made an earnest attempt to study politics when I decided to write this book, simply because of my plan to write a book about Sonia Gandhi. Sonia Gandhi is one of the finest Indian politicians we have amongst us today. India is the largest democracy in the world, and such an Indian politician succeeding in upholding the values of democracy simply means Sonia Gandhi is one of the finest politicians in the world, working within a framework of today's Indian democracy, based on social equality and values.

The word *politics* is derived from *polity* which means 'control' or 'regulation'. Many synonymous terms are in vogue. In modern times, often the common man terms politics as something that is not good or not fair! Common people understand politics only when political exercises affect them adversely. For example, a bad cumulative effect caused by a political policy is considered to happen because of politics itself. This is obviously not true. What is not understood is that, in a democracy, if a policy has failed, the people or the electorate themselves have failed or sometimes the leader fails and these days media is changing the game swinging far and wide with an unpredictable outcome of politics For this reason, one must regard the success of a politician in a democracy as the success as on individually different variables

The best success in politics I love to believe is where a firm clarity of thoughts ideas good faiths and a clear leadership goal with self awareness and self consciousness

In my personal view, Sonia Gandhi's success in her political career derives from the fact that she has been rather judicious and quite a bit more cautious than any of the previous congress presidents or any leader.

Although I could never, in my humble attempt, claim to fully understand what politics is all about, I have worked hard to understand the overview of politics as it relates to the content of this book.

Like any other career, politics is something that people seem to pursue for a variety of reasons. Democracy is a popular form of politics; it is a government that technically is supposed to function to ensure fairness and social equality. Democracy usually is described simply as 'power held by people to ensure the belief of freedom and equality amongst the people'.One can have the best imagination should democracy prevail universally across the world In modern times we may have to call democracy as a good democracy and a bad democracy perhaps

Politics in a democracy like India has always evidenced interest from other parts of the world, and one of the reasons is that women have played a major role in politics in India. Democracy has been surviving in India ever since India gained independence in 1947. This book focuses more on a commoner, Sonia Gandhi(especially a woman adopting a country different from the country of her origin), embracing a career in politics reluctantly yet succeeding in a democratic way that perhaps could be an example of sorts to other people in the world of politics. Sonia Gandhi, it appears, clearly embraced democracy

When she decided to serve Congress, the party her dynastic family of Gandhi-Nehru nurtured for more than half a century. One of the international press releases quotes, 'Sonia Gandhi derived power from being the head of the dynasty.' It perhaps is incorrect to view Sonia Gandhi's power as being derived from her family dynasty alone. Although the influence of the Gandhi-Nehru dynasty can never be underestimated, the power of Sonia Gandhi is solely 'the power of Sonia Gandhi' in my view. There are many facts to support this. First, Sonia Gandhi worked hard and alone and is the most self aware person as it happens. None of the other members of the Nehru-Gandhi family ever trained her or lured her into politics. Second, Sonia Gandhi has always been ever-clear that she was in no race for power or position so her comfort and no rush succeeded. Third, Sonia Gandhi is the most cautious and resilient professional in Indian politics. Fourth, Sonia Gandhi truly embraces the strong values of democracy like any other congressman or congresswoman. Fifth she never expressed, trained or planned into politics and in fact when she met Rajiv Gandhi she had little idea of his background Sixth she declined the highest office though elected to with a thumping majority here the humanity votes humanity as we can safely assume Sixth as she commands the Congress party functioning she continues to work and function without the chair or office as ably and as comfortably and in fact though the most powerful even at the time of writing she has chosen a non Gandhi as the president of Indian National Congress that she served for the longest period of time

The Indian electorate recognized these qualities in Sonia Gandhi, and this is what supported her leadership qualities. The power is not in all derived from being the head of the dynasty. There are innumerable instances of heirs to such dynasties failing miserably across the world. The influence of the Nehru-Gandhi dynasty no doubt is there in Sonia Gandhi, as the family upheld Congress, it would be impossible that she would not to be influenced by her exposure to such a culture. Today's Congress in India exists solely on the shoulders of Sonia Gandhi's dedication and hard work as she upholds and promotes congressional ideals rigidly propelled by the bright promises in Rahul Gandhi and Priyanka Gandhi

The Congress party saw its defeat in the recent 2014 elections. This defeat happened because the party relied on some of the poorest marketing skills amidst the growing influence of social media and split-second electronic communication in India, which also reached out to the Indian diaspora like never before. The Congress party did not make use of social media despite the fact that(Congress Prime Minister Rajiv Gandhi's liberalisation policy India actually pioneered the IT industry advent in India). Sam Pitroda served as a cabinet minister on Public Information Infrastructure and Innovation and spearheaded India's prominence on a global level in the IT industry. Today's Indian IT companies such as Infosys, Wipro, and Tata Consultancy Services (TCS) would not have existed if Pitroda had not initiated his IT liberalization policy. The electorate and the failed results grossly missed the thorough understanding.

I am certain that, with effective marketing of the congress party goals, including effective use of all media, specifically the electronic media, the Congress party will recover,re-emerge or oppose as a dynamic leader in the face of defeat in 2014.

Congress is the only party under the leadership of Sonia Gandhi that harnessed the potential of intellectual minds such as Dr Manmohan Singh, P. Chidambaram, and Sam Pitroda to name a few. It is the only party that harnesses and supports dynamism in the most democratic way possible, and this is nothing but the emergent sole decision of Congress president Sonia Gandhi. It would be incorrect to state that the Congress president ruled the government via the United Progressive Alliance (UPA). What should be inferred is that all congressional ideals and decisions stem from the able leadership of Sonia Gandhi. It would also be incorrect to say the powerful late prime minister Manmohanji was all his own personal credit It must be understood fundamentally it was the decision of Sonia Gandhi to mentor Manmohanji and his position saw enormous presence of India on economic landscape at the time(The technical details of taxation and voluntary disclosure of taxes which set a record is beyond the scope of this part here) Unfortunately this leader Manmohan singh ji is no more by the time of writing this book and all his talent was evident in the landmark economy policies that the UPA chair then led

In a critical review of myself funded review of my originally published book 2016,the critic strongly felt I am under a misapprehension that Sonia Gandhi led the UPA I wish to strongly re-endorse that I stand by that statement in my original book and in its republication in this one without a doubt

Therefore, anything that deserves mention about Congress has to be the result of decisions made by Sonia Gandhi. The electorate who voted for her never simply voted for Sonia Gandhi by virtue of her being a part of the dynasty. Sonia Gandhi has been elected for her unequivocal stand on congress policies. The Indian electorate voted for Sonia Gandhi and never found her Italian birth an issue;

nevertheless, her foreign origin has been questioned – perhaps discriminated against – by some needlessly. The Indian electorate completely forgot Congress amidst a gross lack of marketing and unrealistic expectations in the 2014 elections.

A recent average estimate about GDP growth when and if women in India engage in work is estimated to be a whopping 27 per cent. This compares to a range of 5, 7, and 9 per cent increases in developed countries like the United States of America. The female electorate in India are significant, and their significance on the planet is growing at a fast pace simply by virtue of the numbers of women that exist in India. Even more significant is the fact that these women are mostly young and middle aged(working and training resourceful ages). The Congress I have to mention has been sponsoring existing benefit of free travel, (In Public transport in the state of Karnataka,India) something that does not exist anywhere else in the world The author enjoyed free rides under this scheme in the beautiful city of Bengaluru in India I hereby express my gratitude on behalf of all women who are enjoying this benefit as its a relief to every Indian woman's pinching pockets due to the inflation limiting to the Indian women

Before these significant estimates even came in, Sonia Gandhi's presidency saw an immense push to bring the Women's Reservation Bill before the parliament. I am delighted that the women's reservation bill has been passed and India has a woman president in power at the time of updating this. This bill would reserve 33 per cent of all seats in the lower house of Parliament of India and in all state legislative assemblies for women. I sincerely hope this will set an example across the planet. Women's issues are diverse and complex, as women are suppressed, exploited, and discriminated against. They are very vulnerable. Sonia Gandhi has been a pioneer in the move to emphasise the power of women's presence in the parliament.

It is Sonia Gandhi's visionary ability that pushed the need for the empowerment of women.

Although Sonia Gandhi married into the well-known political family of the late Indira Gandhi her son, the late Rajiv Gandhi, she was, at the time of her marriage, a commoner. She adopted her husband's surname after her marriage to Rajiv Gandhi and pursued the family career in politics singlehandedly after his tragic assassination.

It is a lesser-known fact that there seems to be no apparent relationship of Mahatma Gandhi to the other popularly known Gandhi's including Indira Gandhi, Feroz Gandhi, Sanjay Gandhi, Maneka Gandhi, Varun Gandhi, Priyanka Gandhi, and Rahul Gandhi.

Other than Mahatma Gandhi, who was a leader in Indian independence during British rule, the surname Gandhi is more popularly associated with Indira Gandhi, Rajiv Gandhi, Sonia Gandhi, Priyanka Gandhi, and Rahul Gandhi. These associations are now even more popular than associations to Mahatma's own family. Gandhi is a common Gujurathi(That of or by Gujarat,a south western state of India) surname

Sonia Gandhi is an Italian by birth. She moved to India in 1968, and since then has made India her homeland despite some shocking familial tragedies – the assassinations of Indira Gandhi,Rajiv Gandhi and demise of her brother in law Sanjay Gandhi.

At the time in 1997 she accepted the presidency of the Indian National Congress, Sonia Gandhi had not had any mentorship; neither were any of her dear family members alive to guide her. I hope readers sincerely appreciate that it is clear that Sonia Gandhi accepted the responsibility so that she could serve for the common good of the Indian people, and not for any other oft repeated reason of occupying a chair or position. I can even suspect Sonia Gandhi herself had little to believe she is going to be such a strong leader in her that stands today

Sonia Gandhi explained her choice in a candid interview by a renowned Indian journalist, Shekhar Gupta, on his television show, *Walk the Talk.*

In 1980, Sanjay Gandhi, son of then prime minister Indira Gandhi, died in a plane crash, prompting his brother, Rajiv Gandhi, to enter politics out of a sense of family duty. Sonia Gandhi is referenced to have opposed the move. 'I would rather have my children begging in the streets of Delhi than him becoming a politician,' she once remarked, according to Hamish McDonald of the *Far Eastern Economic Review.*

It is widely believed that Sonia Gandhi shared a good relationship with Indira Gandhi and called her 'Mummy'.

Sonia Gandhi is the only person that Rajiv met and married and the same is true for Sonia Gandhi, Sonia Gandhi met only Rajiv and married only Rajiv. (An American asked me if this means something as it is common for people to change partners ! in the US for e.g and she suggested I remove this phrase I was quick to add it is significant because my understanding is she stood by the person she loved and the party her husband represented even after his demise and yes I can understand people hop parties but phenomenally Sonia Gandhi would accept anyone from other parties something that is noteworthy. Sonia Gandhi accepted the position of Congress president in 1998 and continued till 2022 Though her son Rahul Gandhi accepted to preside as a president briefly he demonstrated that spark but also rightly thought he could present in dynamic roles which he succeeds more than aptly as leader of opposition at the time of writing. The daughter and Congress leader Priyanka Gandhi serves in again dynamic roles currently as a member of Lok Sabha since 2024 Together they bind firmly as Congress legacy

Sonia Gandhi has been the longest-serving Congress president and also the fourth foreign-born president of the Congress party till date. Mallikarjun Kharge now presides over as Congress president since 2022

The Indian National Congress political party was formed by a British man, A. O. Hulme, who was the first president ever for the party.

Sonia Gandhi, as the longest-serving president, also has witnessed the passage of some landmark bills that have traditionally been marketed by the Congress.

A large part of the success of the Congress party is attributed to Sonia Gandhi's presidency and her work. She was well known as a kingmaker when she humbly declined the office of prime minister in 2004. There has been a great debate about why she did not accept the position of prime minister despite pressure from the then-successful Congress party. The media have widely speculated that she did not accept because of the issue of foreign birth, although there is no credible reference to this from the resources available from the public domain.

At the time of this writing Sonia Gandhi has clearly, officially said she declined the office humbly, as it was her conscious decision to listen to 'her inner voice'. With this in mind, I can see no correlation to some incorrect stray statements that she declined the office because of foreign birth. This is a significant matter, albeit a discriminatory one(Though Sonia Gandhi has confirmed she never felt as a foreigner), that was raised by the opposition. There was a reference that declared that a person of foreign origin in the position of prime minister was a potential security risk to India.

Sonia Gandhi has, however, strongly mentioned, in one of her recent strongest-ever speeches, 'When I talk of misery about farmers, my language, my accent, my nationality has been questioned.' She said this during a nationally televised speech in 2014–2015 in India.

One of the references quotes thus: 'In December 1997, Sonia Gandhi announced her intention to campaign on behalf of the Congress Party, hoping to revive its image and establish its position as a favourable alternative to the right-wing Hindu- nationalist Bharatiya Janata Party (BJP). The Gandhi family had represented the Congress Party for years – it was the party the family lived and died for, and Sonia Gandhi could not stand to see it falling apart. In her first campaign speech, Sonia Gandhi addressed her change of heart. Her words are found in Paul Dettman's book *India Changes Course:* "In the years since Rajiv Gandhi left us, I had chosen to remain a private person and live a life away from the political arena. My grief and loss have been deeply personal. But a time has come when I feel compelled to put aside my own inclinations and step forward. The tradition of duty before personal considerations has been the deepest conviction of the family to which I belong".'

It was upon the request of senior congress leaders who recognized problems in the Congress party that Sonia Gandhi finally accepted the role of president. There are no references anywhere to explain any reason other than this for her choice. It appeared a clearly decisive move at the time by Sonia Gandhi. This was six years, seven months, and twenty days after the demise of her husband, Rajiv Gandhi. The senior congress leaders, it appears, had faith in Sonia Gandhi to lead the party(though someone could oppose her,she stabilised rather quickly); clearly she upheld their trust over a record of two successive decades.

I have no hesitation in saying that understanding politics is not easy. There are many elements that contribute to political success. In Sonia Gandhi's case, there are many such elements that I wish to elaborate upon in this book. Perhaps these particular elements have not been mentioned anywhere else.

One of the references quotes thus: 'Sonia Gandhi came into her own and became the passionate political star of the Congress party. Her crowd-pulling ability matched that of her husband and mother in-law – and once she had a crowd gathered, Sonia Gandhi was able to rally them around the party's causes.'

Sonia Gandhi continued as a voice for the Congress party. During the 1998 campaign, she travelled 60,000 kilometres and spoke to 138 constituencies in thirty-four days. In the 1998 election, the Congress party gained only one more seat in parliament than it had in 1996, but the election was still considered a success because pollsters had predicted the party would lose seats that year. In 1999, Sonia Gandhi won a seat in parliament. She encouraged her son's (and daughter duo Priyankagandhi) Bharat Jodo Yathra which aroused a lot of national and international excitement and also partnered some of the yathra.

Sonia Gandhi and Priyanka Gandhi Vadra. Her heartfelt smile of appreciation to her supporters is complemented by her pretty daughter. Sonia Gandhi and Priyanka Gandhi Vadra at a public gathering in Rae Bareli May 28 2015

In publicly published interviews in national media, both televised and printed, and in her campaigns, Sonia Gandhi has been clear in stating why she entered politics and why she delayed her entry into politics.

Despite wide criticism about her language barrier – that she cannot be as fluent as an average Hindi-speaking Indian – the criticism is, in itself, more popular than any issue that has arisen from such a 'barrier'. There has been no apparent issue in communication either within the party or with her association with the Indian electorate. It is well known that she leads the Congress party boldly and commendably; no issue with communication terms exists.

Of the other immediate members of the Gandhian household, Maneka Gandhi and Varun Gandhi, neither have supported the Congress party but I can predict Sonia Gandhi accepting everyone effortlessly into Congress even if it was back and forth funnily enough.

As *The Economist* reported, Sonia Gandhi undertook the risk of death when she accepted the post of congress president. When Sonia did accept the responsibility, she experienced an initial sceptical start, but little did people imagine she would grow to a commendable success as now in 2025 The three family members Sonia Gandhi,son Rahul Gandhi and Priyanka Gandhi now stand stronger though opposing the acting government at the centre

The press was also noted to speculate that a majority of the electorate Indian population does not know that she is not related to Gandhi and perhaps dubbed it a success by default for Sonia. This is incorrect. Sonia Gandhi is a well- known person from the Gandhi Nehru household amidst us today. Traditionally and culturally in India a wedded girl is gifted into the wedded boys family As she was a mother with the responsibility of children on her shoulders with not much noteworthy moral support and perhaps only a potentially suspicious Indian electorate (as *The Economist* reported), I do like to believe it was the most courageous decision

Sonia Gandhi could make a true Indian, and a positive move for all, this along with the fact that she was living the fullest life as an Indian having embraced 'Indianism' at its best.

I shudder to think that Sonia Gandhi gambled with her life at the time she made the bold decision to accept the post of congress president whatever contradiction people may wish to fathom. It is good enough reason to believe that she did this with the best interest of serving India and trying to bring to life the desires of her husband, Rajiv Gandhi, and her mother-in- law, Indira Gandhi.

I believe this simply because Sonia Gandhi did perform surprisingly well as a serving congress president in the years to come. She also won over some critics who wondered if she could survive in the difficult world of politics with so many contrasts and differences she had to face during her tenure.

It is a well-known fact that the success and the charm the Congress party had during her tenure was directly attributable to Sonia Gandhi, and Congress relived some of its lost glory due to Sonia Gandhi.

Sonia Maino was born on 9 December 1946 to Stefano and Paola Maino in Lusiana, in Maini street a historically Cimbrian- speaking village about 35 km from Vicenza in Veneto, Italy. She was one of three siblings: Sonia, Nadia and Anoushka, raised in a traditional Roman Catholic Christian family. Sonia spent her adolescence in Orbassano, a town near Turin. She attained primary education attending the local Catholic schools; one of her early teachers described her as "a diligent little girl, [who] studied as much as was necessary".[19]

Coming from a traditional Italian family and living under the roof of the Gandhi family, she had the best of the two worlds. This, perhaps, helped her win not just because of the name Gandhi, as most critics would have liked to criticise. Also it should be easy to believe she handled the party rather too well with her great skills in management, decision making, impersonal tactics,simplicity, no-nonsense attitude, directorial ability, management of human resources, and great leadership qualities. With regard to her decision making qualities, it is noteworthy and commendable that she consented to the entry of her husband, Rajiv Gandhi, into politics though hesitant.

One leading Indian journalist reported that Sonia Gandhi definitely brought the hitherto fragmenting Congress party together. Another leading Indian journalist stated that she has done little about corruption. In my understanding, it is praiseworthy that she clearly led the flock, and that itself is a task to be praised. When great leadership exists it paves way for reform. Also it is a challenging task to integrate the 'branded Congress party' dramatically as there was a significant seven-year loophole of Gandhi household's complete lack of interference in the party. Sonia Gandhi hailing from common background emphasis common minimum programme led initiatives more to the common masses which is crucial in countries like India

Non Confrontation, perseverance, patience, responsibility are evidently some bigger personal and professional essential attributes in Sonia Gandhi.

While there is a general tendency to seek limelight and seek interviews, as these are seen as marketing gimmicks in Indian politics used to woo the press and voters, Sonia Gandhi remains one of the few successful politicians who has scheduled very few planned interviews till date. Yet she has succeeded in the political output rather powerfully with carefully drafted resourceful messages. Sonia Gandhi has stood the rigour and the dynamics of Indian politics with immense resilience. She focuses on real-time hard work rather than pushing herself into the media (In fact we can observe her avoid if possible My view is that Priyanka Gandhi fills this void in her leadership...Priyanka Gandhi overflows in her capacity to handle media and I have to add there is a neverending potential in Priyanka Gandhi to influence media and masses alike). It is clear that Sonia Gandhi believes that real work is more effective than speeches; however, she never underestimates the presence of her campaigning in times of need. An average voter may be led to think that Sonia Gandhi perhaps does little, while the actual fact is that she shows much more of an executive politician than an oratorical politician.

Despite the dynamism and the tough political atmosphere that comes with her job, it must have been a challenge for Sonia Gandhi to have survived the grit of such an environment

Let alone upholding the political influence that the previous congress presidents had, merely surviving as a congress president could have easily been termed as success for Sonia Gandhi. Indeed, Congress lit up after Sonia Gandhi stepped in.

I like to think that the fact that Sonia Gandhi has harnessed her potential as a political leader has perhaps made her one of the coolest politicians in India. While it was a general opinion amongst critics that language would be a barrier, I like to think it has made her sharper, as it meant harder work to understand the Indians and politics and perhaps made her more successful in dealing with human resources in politics. Language is indeed a perceived barrier for leaders and the electorate alike, especially for leaders who have the responsibility to rule at the central level in a plurilingual democracy like India. Indeed, there are about hundreds of dialects and innumerable castes and subcastes in India(No absolute figures have been deduced at the time of writing). Additionally, the country is an umbrella to all religions of the world.

Social media platforms like you tube have revolutionised access to non English speaking population of the world I hope China, India Russia and Japan invent more and more platforms like youtube to be the voice of Asia Pacific Africa and non English speaking regions of the world All of the broadcast interviews and published interviews by Sonia Gandhi available in the public domain are replete with clear, conscious, and honest explanations of her why's and when's concerning her foray into Indian politics, and they reflect the professionalism necessary for the success of a politician. The message is rather crystal clear to every average Congress believer.

Sonia Gandhi's foreign origin has been needlessly brought to light by the opposition. I like to believe that her Italian upbringing and her life abroad in London have only uniquely helped her success, perhaps not to mention the challenges of being absorbed into Indianism eventually. Sonia Gandhi is an empathic and a considerate politician who, despite her powerful position, reaches out to every necessary grassroots-level Congress worker, many of whom I personally have had an opportunity to interact with.

This has strengthened my ever growing respect for a star politician (or anyone in similar position) Often in the press there are suggestions that her mannerisms in public are akin to those of the late Prime Minister Indira Gandhi; however, my perception, having passively (and actively a real witness)observed Sonia Gandhi in her political presence, especially in the media, is that she has learnt her mannerisms and evolved them beautifully to set a signature of her own. She often wears the traditional *sari*, the Indian traditional draped costume. She wears it with dignity, portraying her interest in the Indian hand-loomed fabrics and handicrafts.

Sonia Gandhi's majestic presence on an international arena is somewhat a matter of pride for many women in India. It is remarkable that a sizable portion of the growing Indian electorate is women voters, and Sonia Gandhi has been mindful of this fact.

Sonia Gandhi has appealed to all congressmen and congresswomen alike by her clear way of conduct and behaviour. She has stood the test of time as a congresswoman with integrity.

It is heartening to see the party workers within Congress show unflinching faith in Madam Sonia, as they affectionately like to address her as they request that she makes the party better. It is perhaps unfair to think it is only the surname Gandhi that has given her success in politics. Sonia Gandhi accommodates congress workers democratically from the entire subcontinent and lends special ears to underprivileged classes in contrast to perhaps a norm that includes powerful leaders who like to favour the corporate 'biggies'. Indeed Sonia Gandhi is an unconventional politician in such respects. 10, Janpath Road her official residence hosts a lot of global celebrities and politicians Sonia Gandhi (INC) favours the lesser privileged yet farming community and common masses trying to step higher in economy ladder

As a leading journalist pointed out, Sonia Gandhi was not dealing with politics in the Indian democracy when her predecessors, Indira and Rajiv, were in office. And the contextualisation in terms of time would have to be different, as Sonia Gandhi is dealing with politics when India is a democracy and has had many challenges to be overcome. It is Sonia Gandhi's leadership policies that shot India into global prominence; not many average voters may appreciate this. Sonia Gandhi led the move on Special Economic Zones (SEZ), a technically superb policy that hardly any parties can appreciate, and this appealed to me. Her policy on genetically modified crops also appealed to me, as this policy during and prior to the leadership of Sonia Gandhi led the United Progressive Alliance to protect farmers' interests. (a significant majority in India which averages about a percentage of 60s and 70s over the last few decades) These technicalities may not have been understood, let alone appreciated by the average Indian person in the electorate. Sonia Gandhi's support of the policies that have overseen and transformed Indian railways, helping the system to be sustained and to survive, is historical. The story of the Indian railways is one of the most successful stories in recent times in the world. This government initiative has been nourished by policies led by Sonia Gandhi over many governments.

Sonia Gandhi's style of working and making decisions, especially with regard to the opposition, particularly lacks extremism or dramatic overtones. Her actions have only helped Congress. Her undeniable secular approach has also appealed to the electorate of all religions and castes alike in Indian politics.

She has appealed to the Hindu electorate as she has ensured family traditions in Hinduism by following all the expected Hindu rituals. A significant number of congressmen and congresswomen who are Muslims have unhesitatingly reassured the Muslim electorate of her universal respect to all. And, as Sonia Gandhi was brought up as a Roman Catholic, it has been rather easy for her to relate to the minority Christian faith amongst other faiths followed in India. Sonia Gandhi is a politician who truly leads a secular life, and she is not just preaching secularism. One may appreciate Sonia Gandhi as a truly secularly executive politician. Seriously with the rate of rapid globalization does it really matter the differences of age, nationality, language etc etc etc ? I wonder in amazement

The choice of Manmohan Singh, who is believed to have been chosen by Sonia Gandhi as prime minister, has appealed to a lot of literate voters and Indians and in some respects restored faith among the Sikh community.

As Sonia Gandhi carved her career in politics, it appears she has seen no need to push herself, as she has moderated her work in human resources and development policies alongside being a responsible mother to India's most certain current and future political leaders, her children, Priyanka Gandhi and Rahul Gandhi, both of whom are now executing significant roles within the congress to help their beloved mum. This has re-established that the business of politics is definitely a family tradition in the Gandhi trio rather than a pathless ambition.

Priyanka Gandhi, the pretty daughter politician of Sonia Gandhi, is usually in the limelight all too often. She grabs the newspaper headlines and the average Indian's attention rather too easily. Priyanka Gandhi is no doubt a charming and beautiful politician amidst us. Huge pressure was imposed on pulling Priyanka Gandhi into mainstream politics at the young age of twenty-five. Sonia Gandhi's reaction is quoted in one of the references: 'She is only twenty-five." She meant that her daughter was too young to be pulled into mainstream politics. Priyanka Gandhi is a successful Congress Leader at the time of writing and offers 'sit up to watch' leader styled speeches to oppose the acting government and a real leader meeting and influencing public realtime and on media .She leaves no stone unturned

In a televised interview by one of the Indian press reporters with Priyanka Gandhi, Priyanka effortlessly and clearly explained her respect for Sonia Gandhi's role in politics and her reasonable comfort in vocalising in Hindi, the national language of India.She follows the footsteps firmly and decisively plunging into fighting into elections and managing the affairs of the party all round at the time of this publication in 2025

It is widely reported that Sonia Gandhi has always been a very family-oriented person, and her main focus in life has always clearly been her family. It is believed that a strong sense of family is common to both Italian and Indian cultures

Being Italian in her origin, she must have experienced a major transformation from Italianism to Indianism. Sonia Gandhi has done this rather believably, and it is known from her close sources that she is comfortable with the North Indian staple food, which is *dhal* (lentils) and *roti* (staple Indian bread), for her routine. Having married into the Gandhi household and worked for the Gandhi household, she carries their purpose and tradition forward naturally.

The family sacrifices in the deaths of Rajiv Gandhi and Indira Gandhi did not sway the devotion of Sonia Gandhi against the family values of the Nehru-Gandhi dynasty.

It is noteworthy that there are many successful Indian politicians who cannot communicate in English or Hindi who still find it difficult to address public gatherings, let alone scheduled interviews. One such former prime minister of India had to work hard to learn Hindi soon after he assumed the office of prime minister. Hindi is the widely prevalent national language of India. This was never an issue with Sonia Gandhi.

With the Indian democratic secular voter in focus, nothing other than a clear choice of the politician matters, and in some respects Sonia Gandhi's political success is a testament to this. The electorate voted for Sonia Gandhi and her strongly democratic policies in spite of her family sacrifices – Shri Rajiv Gandhi and Indira Gandhi.

Sonia Gandhi is generally an intensely private person, and her privacy was always especially respected by Rajiv Gandhi and the Gandhi household. However, her entry in politics meant that she had to open herself up. Some notice has been made of her apparent initial discomfort in addressing meetings, rallies, and other public events. It certainly did not take her long to shed that largely private image, as Sonia Gandhi is well aware she is part of the general public. It is well known that Sonia Gandhi reciprocates the electorate rather naturally. She doesn't rely on gimmicks. She doesn't issue needless press releases or seek paparazzi. She is not at all ostentatious. She has been adept in steering her family matters from catching undue attention. The very few official press releases from Sonia Gandhi's office are earnest and carefully framed.

There has been a lot of criticism that Sonia Gandhi perhaps does not open up and is an intensely private person. My perception, which may agree with how an average electorate thinks, is that she does enough to maintain the moderation with regard to marketing her decisions for the Congress's policies. Difficulties can arise when ideas and proposed policies are over publicized. Perhaps Sonia Gandhi more than appreciates that.

No single politician I know of has had such an immediate exposure to politics than Sonia Gandhi. Sadly, her exposure was instigated by two brutal assassinations in the Gandhi family and the demise of SanjayGandhi not excluded. But, whether she was an aspiring politician or not, she lived under one roof with successful politicians, and perhaps her observation of their good works helped her when she actively took part in politics herself.

Under Sonia Gandhi's leadership, the Congress functions absolutely democratically with careful decisions made about governance at a regional level and central level. This decision making is not always easy, and democracy is the key to Sonia Gandhi's executive style of functioning.

A lot of the success of the Congress party today undoubtedly is Sonia Gandhi's hard work; the charm of the name *Gandhi* is undoubtedly here to stay.

It is believed that Sonia Gandhi completed an art restoration course from the National Gallery of Modern Art. She has received honorary doctorates from many universities including Aligarh Muslim University, University of Brussels, and Madras University.

In a significant interview with one of the leading press reporters, Sonia Gandhi was fairly open regarding her entry into Indian politics. There need be no better clarity of her intention to serve in the best interests of the Congress. I find Sonia Gandhi's life a good example, and I wish to elaborate as much as my view and understanding permits.

It was necessary for me to understand more about politics, as I have had no exposure to politics. All my life I wished to be a health care professional, maybe a doctor and my humble beginnings as an average Indian education product ; I wanted only to pursue a career in medicine. However, now I wish to establish a portfolio of writing. After starting a career in family practice, I was forced to refine my communication skills; I needed the skills so I could appropriately convey my ideas and thoughts.

This career in medicine led me to travel to many countries, and I have been amazed at how important clear communication is for the conveying of thoughts.

Even so, I learnt that politics within my own profession, much as national politics and international politics, did seem to play an unhealthy unexpected role – just as it does in the higher levels of politics. I must confess that I worked hard to stay away from such politics; I did not want to get entangled in such impish games. My little understanding is that politics is a part and parcel of everyone's life; this is the rule rather than the exception. It was during the dull moments in my career between 2013 and 2015 that I chose to read about Sonia Gandhi, this politician rising inexplicably from tragedies that befell her family. I was inspired to write about her phenomenal achievements. I found many underlying inspiring facts in my research into Sonia Gandhi and politics in general; and I found I was determined to book a constructive takeaway of her biopic.

Indeed, I found a role model in Sonia Gandhi. She travelled away from her country of origin without an iota of thought that she might have to carry the legacy of a responsible position in politics someday. (I also support another celebrity Meghan Markle who has had a taste of difficulty in accommodating to a different nationality,I believe we must support rather than criticise or discriminate ,we must welcome rather than scare the hell out of people who adopt different countries. we must love than hate. Peace love and harmony succeeds slow yet sure and certain) I present a rather focussed commoner's understanding of politics in this book (focus on women adopting a different nation and I love to mention the first lady of the United States Melania Trump). These women are to be loved, supported and their positions welcomed as they belong to us as one.

Although I could never, in my humble attempt, fully know how politics swings into action, I do realize that, in the modern world, many people enter politics in an effort to lead and govern a country, but their motives or agendas more often than not is simply a race for personal power. A career in politics does not always seem to direct people to 'achieve a clean governance' or to actually use power cautiously or to regulate a community or nation effectively.

Like any other career, politics to govern a country or a community is something that people seem to pursue for a variety of reasons. Politics in a democracy like India has always evidenced interest elsewhere because women have played a major role in Indian politics as much as they have across the globe. Why am I specifying women? Women are so often oppressed. They are discriminated against. Women have their rights crushed often. It is a widespread narrative that women are weak and vulnerable. The list of reasons do not seem to end. This has been the scenario at least in a large part of Asia, Asia Pacific and Africa where there is little respect and consideration for women, and they are not encouraged to uphold their own dignity. It may seem far-fetched, yet so many women face economic and educational barriers not to forget Africa and remote tribals of the inaccessible world

In fact, women are often classed amongst the weaker segments in a developing country like India. The levels of training, literacy, and self-reliance are more often at the lowest levels on an economic ladder. This fosters a vicious circle of exploitation, abuse, discrimination, and in turn, hinders any progress of economic development. Women face enormous challenging situations in life because of the dynamics of their own bodies, which contributes to how they are perceived in a society ... grossly discriminated against in my view. Women are less empowered as they cannot be at work while they are burdened with the responsibility of motherhood. Hence my sincere message is that any woman who succeeds in a career needs enormous respect, as such a woman has seemingly worked consistently against such barriers of gender, language, culture, nationality ... and the list again seems endless.

Sonia Gandhi has constantly stood up for the good cause of the empowerment of women along with the empowerment of many other less-privileged classes in India. I find this most endearing. Her work in this cause appears like an oasis in a desert for the grossly neglected class of women in India. No politician other than Sonia Gandhi has stood up for this noble cause in recent times in the history of politics in India. Sonia Gandhi continues to do so despite opposition and odds to ensure that women are empowered

The first time I developed intense admiration for Sonia Gandhi was when I was in my early twenties in the late eighties and I visited a government outlet called Karnataka Chitrakala Parishat on Race Course Road in Bangalore, South India. I found myself attracted to the hand-loomed saris that had been woven by the tribes and rural men and women in India. I admired the exquisite hand-loomed fabrics that were made into saris, but the particular designs worn by Sonia Gandhi seemed to be my favourite. I was touched when I learned that these were specially sponsored by Sonia Gandhi's affiliates. The folks who wove these beautiful saris had been funded through Sonia Gandhi's sponsorship. I was pleased to learn this from the artisans who directly sold their handmade goods in this outlet. This, I thought, is what makes this woman a genuinely good politician. She had served as a real example by conducting fair trade that contributed to the welfare of the poor artisans and tribes in India.

I applied to the Chinese based Yidan Foundation (https://yidanprize.org/2020 and 2021 consecutively) to hypothesise policy models to empower women.I appealed by my 40 page worth of hypothesis and application to make education and higher education free for women across the world I appealed to all governments of the world to provide free,nontaxable STEM(Science Technology Engineering and Medicine education and higher education to every women across the world) I appeal to the whole world education increase opportunities part time and apprenticeships and training and employment be parttime world wide so the output can be greater than never before because maternity and paternity roles have reversed and women can find it hard to achieve full potential with full time training,motherhood and caring responsibility and lack of tax subsidies and lack of sponsorships to women girl children and girl babies care. Men can then see greater levels of satisfaction without a doubt Time is shrinking and decision making needs to become innovative and futuristic and dynamic These are exclusively my views not mentioned or thought of by any one else other than myself ever simply because I had a devastating blow to a lot of my roles because of lack of acknowledgment I appeal to every medical and nursing college provide free education to every girl across the world,the beneficiary is the society more than the girl herself

In India the artisans from remote, rural, and tribal areas need marketing support to enhance their productivity. This has been actively provided by Sonia Gandhi's affiliates, and continues even today. This is something the Congress party stands by – supporting underprivileged rural folk and the weaker economic sections of society. Education amongst girls and women is below that of boys and men worldwide especially Asia Asia Pacific and Africa The irony of the developed countries is women will have to still juggle between caring responsibility and career and often thankless jobs with no pay, no taxation free or incentives of any kind ever ! Women at the time of writing compete with men on a single pedestal though women at all times would have performed two jobs for the price of one (sometimes no pay for either woefully) women with potential motherhood responsibilities continue in employment and earn stress as a byproduct along with loss of health,security, job and wellbeing is nowhere close!

When I was a medical student in my early twenties, the face of Sonia Gandhi in the media in India always made me feel for her. What were those feelings? Why did they emerge? I simply could not understand the overly critical remarks about Sonia Gandhi. Those thoughts remained in my heart … and I put my thoughts aside, perhaps to revisit at some time later in my life.

I am pleased to say I have been able to write down my thoughts about a real woman achiever we have today in the world – Sonia Gandhi. This book is very special to me, and I hope it will be special to many readers who appreciate the content that focuses on Sonia Gandhi's dedication to the Indian National Congress party, and in particular, her strong stand for unity, tolerance, and freedom.

Sonia Gandhi works tirelessly to promote the ideals and causes of the Congress. She was accepted as the president partly at the request of hundreds of congressmen and congresswomen from across India because they have faith and trust in her, and partly because of a responsibility that she wished to shoulder. In an official Indian press release she wrote, 'It would have been cowardly of me not to have accepted to help the Congress party when Congress leaders approached me explaining the difficulties that Congress party then was facing, and this is why I came in.'

There have been references to some significant opposition from Sonia Gandhi's own party workers. This is, indeed, the variable face of politics where different ideologies in the form of opposition, should be expected. Sonia Gandhi and the party itself did not yield to such situations because they would have destabilised the initiatives of the Congress. These opposing and testing conditions only strengthened her position, as by mere virtue of her decisions, they were well taken care of. The result was the strengthening of the party's stand on such issues. This is the way every other issue is dealt with democratically by Sonia Gandhi. Her grace and dignity in such times are commendable. Sonia Gandhi is as poised in success as she is while destabilising forces that question her without a fair and valid basis.

There remains no doubt that today's Congress party stands firmly(growing also on the shoulders of Rahul Gandhi and Priyanka Gandhi) on the multifaceted mentorship of Sonia Gandhi's. There have been critical remarks suggesting that she interfered in Dr Manmohan Singh's United Progressive Alliance (UPA) function, but this should be deemed an inaccurate observation. All Congress as well as congress allies function solely with the powerful decisions and dedication provided by Sonia Gandhi as she leads the Congress party. So to then concur that UPA was 'interfered with' is an inaccurate term, as without Sonia Gandhi's presidency, UPA could simply not have existed let alone functioned. The UPA policies shot India's prominence and economy to a standard never before reached in the politics of India at a global level. An unbelievable GDP growth was registered by India when a looming recession plagued the dynamics of the economy of the rest of the world, and this is to be understood as the carefully drafted economic policies by think tanks consisting of people like P. Chidambaram and Dr Manmohan Singh. Perhaps no other party or average member of the electorate can comprehend this. P. Chidamabarm and Dr Manmohan Singh's potential was enhanced by the virtue of the power of the decisions of Sonia Gandhi.

The next time I was pleased was when Sonia Gandhi was voted significantly by *Forbes* magazine as one of the top hundred most powerful women. I was pleased that power rests with such a woman politician of principles who shuns using her power for wrong reasons. In 2004 Sonia Gandhi was voted third most powerful woman in the world. She was third only next to two other celebrated politicians, Condoleazza Rice of the United States and Wu Yi of China. For Sonia Gandhi, this honour represented her part in the power of democracy – the power of leading for a noble cause without actually occupying the coveted office of prime minister. She maintained the power to lead social causes for the greater good in society, and the power to consistently lead a political party in the world's second-largest populated nation.

One of the main attributes *Forbes* took into account was Sonia Gandhi's ability to influence media presence. Her presidency of the Congress party in India, the largest democratic power, was no doubt the example of the 'power' position that the magazine recognized. Sonia Gandhi, in my view, does not work on this control of media presence. It appears that it comes from her nature and her personality. She does not seek to 'market' her hard work; that is, the policies and ideals of Congress. She is an unconventional politician in that sense. Even at the time of writing, Sonia Gandhi remains one of the top one hundred most powerful women on the planet as per the listings of *Forbes* magazine.It must be noted that all this was in a pre-social media era

Sonia Gandhi was a 'reluctant politician' according to *The Economist.*

I just wondered to myself how magical it would be if I could actually meet Sonia Gandhi. I am just a commoner, and she is a celebrity politician; however, I did not wish to believe that my meeting with She could merely be a myth. I was keen to know more and more about her. Sonia Gandhi's personality simply enticed me to meet her no matter what. I felt a little sad at times reading a lot of biased critical comments about her in the press. I had written a book by now, and sometime in 2013 I was keen to consider writing about a woman achiever from India. At this time I was pursuing postgraduate medical training in the United Kingdom, and many faces caught my attention as the possible subject for a book about such a consummate persona. The rigid criteria I had chosen was that the person should have been an Indian celebrity at the global level and have done some significant work that should be applauded at the global level.

Why did I choose India?

India is the largest democracy. Having been born and brought up in such a democratic system, I felt that fundamental human rights, like right not to be discriminated against on the basis of gender, would have paved the way for such a female personality from India to develop the potential for the larger good of the society and world at large.

This is something that persuaded me to consider a woman's personality. Gentleman achievers from India and outside of India, I hope, will respect this. Simply put, women in India are discriminated against because they are women. Hence, gender is potentially a barrier for any woman to achieve her potential. It is my belief that women in India do not enjoy this fundamental human right of not being discriminated against even today. Women continue to be discriminated against globally by everyone else, but that is something that deserves to be addressed elsewhere. I have been discriminated against. I am embarrassed to confess. I was told things like 'Do not worry. You are not growing to be a man. Your work is not that important *because you are a woman.*

This affected my self-esteem and confidence. I was gutted, but I worked on it. I believe that discrimination has severe negative effects on people.

The few prominent globally noteworthy women personalities from India are the Indian beauty queen Aishwarya Rai Bacchan; the CEOChief Executive Officer of Pepsi Company, Indra Nooyi; and Sonia Gandhi. In 2007 I attempted to contact Aishwarya Rai Bachchan via her manager, Simone Sheffield, but I was informed her mother wishes to write about her and therefore she likes to reserve that thought.

The fascination of these three influential women achievers seemed to linger in my mind. The meteoric rise of their careers, though they had emerged from common, ordinary backgrounds, caught my attention.

My busy job in medicine did not permit me any more time, but I began to think seriously about Sonia Gandhi. Although thinking is the easy bit. Even to consider bringing out a fabulous book befitting her celebrity status as a powerful politician, I thought, would be challenging indeed for a common, ordinary, unknown person like me living thousands of miles away from her. And at that point, I had not even thought about even trying to contact her.

Sonia Gandhi, unlike most celebrity personalities, is a person who comes across not overtly wishing to portray the fact that she is indeed a celebrity, and I feel that is unique in her.

How would my plan to meet Sonia Gandhi happen? Would this meeting with her happen? So many questions arose. Most importantly I wished to write about the real power in this fabulous person that should include my views expressly, views that perhaps no one either observed or wished to write about. Unlike a political analyst or critic I believe I might be able to express my views of this famous politician as a commoner.

For some reason I felt it was taboo to write about the constructive side of Sonia Gandhi. Initially I wondered if the press failed to highlight the constructive attributes. I often wondered if there was a misunderstanding involving the dedication that Sonia Gandhi has for the Congress party.

The press enjoys certain liberties and consideration must be given to what they write and say; however, I believe that Sonia Gandhi simply could not be portrayed in her authentic best in the press. It unfortunately is a fact I simply failed to understand. If anything, I became more determined to expressly expose the inspiring best in Sonia Gandhi.

One fine day I thought of writing about her. I had a short, crispy chat with a person I trust, who seemed to be in agreement with my dream of writing a book about her. It was not an easy proposition, as I had a young family to fend for. I was living abroad in England, and

I was going through a challenging time in my career as a professional doctor. But this idea kept me sustained as I faced my challenges simply because, during the dull moments in my career, I enlivened myself by reading about Sonia Gandhi. This was between 2013 and 2015. I worked hard to conceptualize what I was going to write about this phenomenal politician. My view is entirely derived from my own observation and an in-depth analysis after reading a vast set of references that were available at London's British Library. I browsed through the available references and came to know about forty books written about Sonia Gandhi. These exclude thirty-odd more books not archived in the British Library; these books were published and released in India.

All in all, this was the first time I learnt that about sixty books have been written about Sonia Gandhi. It was a lovely task to delve into this documentation; nevertheless, it was a memorable experience that filled me with awe.

The number of books about Sonia Gandhi is significant because it is more than the number of books about other members of the Gandhi dynasty, and I believe deservedly so. I mean no disrespect to the other Gandhi family members, but this simply shows how very popular Sonia Gandhi has been and perhaps will always be. This, in some way, should silence the critics who perhaps think Sonia Gandhi's success is primarily due to her name – that her success is simply because she married into a famous and successful political family.

A large number of books on this list were not in circulation; hence, the only place I could obtain them was at the British Library in London. This is one of the largest libraries in the world. The process to procure all these books was that the British Library gives preference to readers in London and those who actually present themselves personally to the library. The system was that I had to reserve the books I needed at least six weeks in advance(in case I was from outside of London), and then I needed to personally visit the library and do all of my research there.

Sometime in September 2014, I decided it would be a good idea to reserve about thirty books at one time. Readers will appreciate the most tempting fact: Each time I tried to reserve a book about Sonia Gandhi, I discovered that at least three readers every day also wanted to read about Sonia Gandhi. Almost every day for a good few months, I discovered that many citizens of the United Kingdom wanted to know more about Sonia Gandhi.. This I found to be an inspiring fact to share with my readers. The popularity of books about Sonia Gandhi simply showed how popular she enjoys. This is a fact I declare with pleasure, as it strongly supported my idea of writing about her.A certain element of curiosity always grows when it comes to Sonia. I am surprised at what politics can offer pleasantly as most Doctors traditionally either are poor administrators or not at all interested in politics. No doubt I was quick to understand that, if politics has to succeed at a central level, politics has to thrive at the grassroots level. This would be the voters' level where there should be an active participation of voters in the politics that affect them. Here is where I think politics can succeed. I consider myself to be at the grassroots level in politics. It is important that I make an attempt to understand how this all works so I can then take the responsibility to criticize or support particular politicians and their policies and opinions.

So my interesting journey of gathering the prevailing common information so I could put it into a book continued. I made my way to the British Library in London to glean all the classic references. As I learned more and more, I could not help but sit there in awe of Sonia Gandhi. My initial view was that, in reality, the books may not have touched the attributes of the real politician in her. I sat reading those references and found it simply enchanting and interesting to read about Sonia Gandhi. I just did not wish to take breaks for lunch or tea, as I believed they would interrupt the continuing thrill of the moment as I learned about the highlights and milestones of Sonia Gandhi's life that have made history in politics. One day, I just thought I should reminisce about what I had been reading, rather than continue to read, so I piled all the books I had been looking at that day on my allotted table, and off I went to a busy Indian restaurant near the Euston Station in central London. There lay an exotic, heavy Indian buffet. I was a first-time visitor; however, I felt that most of the others there were local regulars. It was pretty busy, as it was clear that the food was popular. Seats were first come first served, and the place was cramped, so that meant that seats had to be shared. I happened to be given a seat opposite a lady who was a Bengali Londoner. She seemed to be in her late fifties. When we started chatting, I disclosed My dream is to read the archives describing Sonia Gandhi's life and achievements, and then write up my own thoughts in a book form. She seemed super thrilled, and agreed with my opinion that Sonia Gandhi is perhaps the most misunderstood person! I was bold and courageous to state with strong conviction that I was sincerely working hard to change such misunderstood views in my book. She wished me luck. We exchanged friendly banter about many issues of Indian politics, and the relative interest in that topic amongst the non-resident Indians, especially those who were based in the United States and Canada, as well as the United Kingdom.

I was appalled at how less informed the non-resident Indians were about the governance in India than the resident Indians. This, perhaps, is because of lack of contact with the home country in India, and this is true of most people like me

With increasing social media influence and globalisation the reach is now getting closer and closer. In 2025, a rough estimate of the number of Indians living outside the country is around 35 million. The Indian diaspora, however, does play a futuristic role without a doubt, I believe, on the national and international political interests that focus India. I felt somewhat embarrassed when I realized that I myself was ignorant about many such issues until I chose to write this book.

I had a lot of friendly chats with a wide variety of people from many diverse backgrounds, and I found it really interesting to hear what everyone thought of Sonia Gandhi, and what they thought about me wishing to write a book about Sonia Gandhi.

A European national in England in her early fifties asked me sometime in 2015, 'Oh, Sonia Gandhi. Is she the daughter of Indira Gandhi?' Wow, I could not help but laugh at her understanding, although I must admit she was not sure. But what may have led her to think Sonia Gandhi as the daughter of Indira? There are two possibilities. Either she got confused between daughter and daughter-in-law, or she struggled with the English language. I reasonably ruled out both, and I asked her why she thought Sonia Gandhi could be the daughter of Indira. She felt that the personalities of Sonia Gandhi and Indira Gandhi were similar; so much so that, hypothetically, they could be mum and daughter. That did leave me with a lovely feeling, because a relationship of this kind should be important. I certainly did not wait to instantly say to her, 'Well, you may wish to read my book, *Sonia Gandhi: The Power Part One* by Roopa Venktesh.' I was somewhat relieved she did not mention Javier Morro's *The Red Sari*. This book is a fictionalised version of Sonia Gandhi's life. Her own response to this book in an official press release is, 'It is sad that someone could do this.' Javier Morro is a Spanish author. I can confirm that I have not read this book. I have no intention of reading any fictionalised and apparently 'sad' matter about Sonia Gandhi.

This conversation led me to Sonia Gandhi's interview with Shekhar Guptaji, renowned Indian journalist, on his New Delhi–based TV show *Walk the Talk*. In the interview, Sonia Gandhi declared her warm sentiment to Mrs Indira Gandhi … crossing language barriers and nationality barriers, so I felt the European national had made a likeable mistake, but I am absolutely chuffed to have to say so. I hereby hope to get in touch with this reader Elena Isherwood,a lovely Spanish teacher.

Here is another snapshot of one of my interviews. I spoke with my neighbour, an alumnus of my school and college. He lives in London and is in his mid-forties. He knows I had written a book before, and he had also learnt that I was now intending to write about Sonia Gandhi. He and I spoke for about an hour, and all that I could learn from him was the hugely prevalent misinformation. I defended continuously as I had credible references to quote. He rather seemed to resolve my views, but with difficulty. I concluded our interview by saying, 'I really hope you read my book, because you will learn that all that you understand is untrue.' This only made me feel all the more determined. This reader in London asked me to consider writing about Modiji instead. He was sure I would succeed .

Another of my respected classmates also contradicted a lot of what I was intending to write in my book. He rather seemed to discourage me, yet after a long debate, he only seemed to conclude, 'Your book might sell, as I know you write well.' Although I was flattered, I wished to keep my writing skills aside. I wished only to focus on Sonia Gandhi and her attributes and nothing else. This placed a responsibility on my shoulders with regard to the matter I wished to publish to uphold the credible references about Sonia Gandhi as best as I could. A strong memorable feedback from a classmate precious view k is that the best parts of this book is entirely the part about me and what do I intend to next etc because my profession in medicine is not even connected remotely to politics (True to this classmate's precious view ,the publisher chose to put my profile photo on cover page instead of Sonia Gandhi's ,I wait to see the reaction of the audience to this with bated breath !)

I had a significant chat with another person whose spontaneous and appealing view was, 'I fully endorse your idea of writing about Sonia Gandhi, as she is a real achiever in seeing her achievements with her family. I can support you to the best of my ability.' Here I had the type of support that I wished for. It would have been simply impossible for me to pursue my plan – my dream plan of writing about Sonia Gandhi – without this support. The general view I gleaned, however, having spoken to a variety of people from across all walks of life and nationalities, was a genuine warm sentiment amongst all people of varied languages,culture,races,and nationalities

My children and I visited India in 2014 where I successfully re-established an old family link with one of the trusted respected congressman who kindly accommodated my request: 'Please, can you Help me meet Sonia Gandhi? I am pretty determined to write about her as I find her inspiring.' The first sentence he uttered was, 'Yes, I can see why you are touched by her work. At the peak of achievement in politics, she has humbly declined to hold the powerful office of prime minister. It is something that not everyone could think of doing.' This congressman was a hardworking, dedicated person, and I found it uncomfortable to upset his busy schedule, yet he was kind, and I hoped he could help me. Somewhere my mind also said, *Be prepared to be disappointed*, as anything can fail in the real world.

We returned to England after this vacation in India. I kept my rigorous schedule of trying my best.I chased up nonstop on a fortnightly basis One fine day in late April 2015, I set out for New Delhi where Sonia Gandhi lives and works. Indeed it appeared plausible that I could dare to dream. I had not the faintest idea how the system of appointments with Sonia Gandhi worked; in fact, I had no idea how Indian politics functions in the lanes of 10 Janpath, the official residence of Sonia Gandhi, or at the Parliament House or any other part of the government.

Every day seemed uncertain, as I understood Sonia Gandhi really is a very hardworking politician. There is a long queue indeed of people waiting to meet her. A trusted person from Sonia Gandhi's office declared that there have been instances in which appointments are oversubscribed and postponed disappointingly. One fine day I got a call – that magical call – allowing my ordinary self to meet Sonia Gandhi. Understandably, it was to take place at the Parliament House.

I simply could not believe my ears, and I paid great attention as I dressed myself; anything I considered seemed too insignificant, and yet I hopelessly tried to work out, *Is this important? Should I do this?* I was too overwhelmed. I also seemed to reflect on Sonia Gandhi's impeccable dress style, which has always been highly rated in her career. She favours cool traditional and simply fabulous traditional Indian costumes … something that beats the greatest Indian fashion makers' dream. And over the last decade, fashion makers from India have assumed global importance. Sonia Gandhi is often seen dressed in shades of white White is a colour used to suggest calming or peace, non violence and can suggest something pure perhaps absolute purity.

Indeed, I believe that Sonia Gandhi's traditional Indian wear is the best and never fails to impress any Indian and anyone outside India.

Sonia Gandhi is someone who sees her comfort in the traditional, time-tested, and ever-fresh-looking sari, a traditional six-foot-long wrapped costume worn by most Asian women in India, Pakistan, Bangladesh, Srilanka, and Indonesia. So much that is India is obvious in Sonia Gandhi.

I chose the comfortable *salwar kameez*, a traditional north Indian costume. My appointment was for ten o'clock in the morning. It was sunny and warm as I approached the superb pink Parliament (British architecture) House. It is a beautiful, stunning, and imposing building. This was my first ever visit to the Parliament House At the time of writing a new parliament house is being built for custom.. With my three five years studying Sanskrit while doing my O and A levels, I recognized the inscription as I looked above on the ceiling, very close to the main entrance just before I could actually enter the hall. The inscription in Sanskrit, in Devanagari script, says, roughly, 'Where there be respect … righteousness may prevail.' The word for 'righteousness' here is *dharma*, which in Sanskrit refers to a righteousness of a high order as prescribed by ancient Hindu scriptures. I stood there hopelessly memorizing this sentence. Surely, Sanskrit appeals to me anytime because I am a practising Hindu singing hymns of our Hindu Gods and deities. No pens or mobile phones were allowed, so I had to rehearse the inscribed sentence over and over in my mind, even though I was sure I would also be able to find this quote from our primary Hindu scriptures, the Upanishads or the Vedas, or from the *smritis*, which are secondary scriptures.

The security procedure was long and tedious. My credentials were checked in. Three officers had apparently signed the entry ticket. And I again had to go through three more chambers before I finally went into the huge building.

My heart fluttered at the thought of what I should say. *How do I start?* Anyway, I went in, and I will never forget the warm smile of Sonia Gandhi that welcomed me.

My initial impression forced me to love this utterly down-to-earth great human being, Sonia Gandhi, who set a classic example for all of us on the planet by turning down power with unbelievable charm so she could *simply work* for the betterment of the people, especially the weaker and less empowered. Her gentle, caring and compassionate voice quickly impressed me. I literally froze at the aura that struck me.

Before I had even thought about developing my idea to write a book, I had accessed information in the public domain to appreciate the demeanour of Sonia Gandhi. I had watched many televised interviews. In them, she appeared formal, yet she carefully conveyed the all- important message regarding her position as the president of the Indian National Congress. I was quick to note that my own interview was far more amazing. Perhaps this was because it was somewhat informal, but all I could infer was there was no doubt that this great politician I had read about extensively at the British Library and elsewhere fitted my imagination of a fabulous politician with decades of experience with the power of a silent winner in politics for such a significant period of decades that perhaps no one may ever I appreciate it. This is because Sonia Gandhi is one of the rare politicians who has delivered more and spoken less, and this appears to be her style of functioning and her remarkable trait. The contrary seems to be true about most of the successful parties in which political manifestos are hyped up and little or nothing may be delivered.

The congressman introduced me to Sonia Gandhi as a doctor who was her admirer and who had come to visit her. A typical mother, Sonia Gandhi, first asked, 'What about your parents? Where do they live?' I told her they lived there in India. The first thing I think I said was, 'It is amazing what you are doing, ma'am.' This was my heartfelt congratulations, which I spontaneously expressed. She said, humbly, 'Well, we are trying!' Reflecting back on this, I thought *trying* was perhaps the appropriate term for about two decades worth of her intense determination, hard work, and resilience in politics! She humbly seemed to collectively refer to all the congressmen together as she used the word *we*. She showed no air of superiority whatsoever. My initial view was that those were carefully chosen words for a seasoned politician in dark contrast to the words of a flabbergasted amateur writer like me. I remarked about the unpleasant misinformation that prevailed about politics in India in general, and I said to her, 'I would like to write something good about you.' I also mentioned to her that I was too excited to say anything! She replied, 'I do not want to interrupt what you are doing.' Her truly democratic response to me was simply great. She mentioned her own book, which I had already read. It was published by Penguin India. Sonia Gandhi did not seem to be keen on marketing or endorsing any of my ideas, which I expected as a result of my meticulous study. I can confirm that this person showed enormous eloquence, grace, dignity, and respect. I had a fascinating conversation with Sonia Gandhi.

The most prominent statement of the conversation, which I think we all should reflect upon, is this: 'Hatred is something that should never be encouraged, and training and teaching people to hate another human being on any basis such as a community is something that should never be encouraged.' This message stands strongly. This is something Sonia Gandhi obviously felt so deeply about that she expressed it to me in this appointment. Therefore, it is something I invite every reader to ponder upon. I am sure every one of us will agree this is something we all can inculcate to make the world a better place to live in. We must all stop hatred on any basis or characteristic.

I became a doctor because I have a natural heart to heal a suffering person. Because of this, Sonia Gandhi's message touched a strong chord in my heart, and it was my thought to perhaps stand by her for this message no matter what, when, where, or how. These heartfelt thoughts simply appealed to me more than anything she said. Imagine a world that carries no trace of any hatred amongst humanity. Such a fabulous heaven in the making that would be. It is my fantasy that we could make that happen in the world. As a mere fantasy, it was simply superb. Is it possible ? Nothing is impossible! I love to believe that the world cannot wipe off these hurdles of widespread hatred with only a single person – Sonia Gandhi – working hard against such forces. We must all pitch in! I welcome every reader to encourage this move to *stop hatred! I invite each of you to join me on https://www.facebook.com/profile. php?id=100008570314889*

https://www.instagram.com/roopavenktesh7/

https://studio.youtube.com/channel/UCpiDRj_NgZV2o1DRVX3Bepw/ videos/upload?filter=%5B%5D&sort=%7B%22columnType%22%3A% 22date%22%2C%22sortOrder%22%3A%22DESCENDING%22%7D

Towards the end of our meeting, I was so excited I could not seem to think anymore or to react. Before I realized how fast this magical The appointment had come to an end, Sonia Gandhi stood up. I stood back and bowed to her. Her reciprocation was just so gracious. I had just experienced an unbelievable milestone in my life. I had met with a stunning democrat who had appealed to my democratic sense during this fabulous appointment. The experience will remain very special for me I believe! I did not make any notes during our appointment. I retired back to where I lived in Karnataka Bhavan, Chanakya Puri, New Delhi, and I made my own notes of recollection of the meeting. It was a fantastic moment I shall cherish forever.

I was reeling in excitement. As a matter of fact, the excitement will always linger. I am in awe of this wonderful personality, Sonia Gandhi, who works amongst us tirelessly behind the scenes with a special dedication and tenacity.

Much of her work goes to help the less empowered sections of society like women and other oppressed classes while not sacrificing the interests of the other sections of the society. She is well aware, especially, that many women may have been discriminated against and therefore sadly robbed of their potential to achieve the fullest potential in society. This is a notable attribute, and I found that none of the books I read elaborated on it. Remarkably, Sonia Gandhi does not mention this or promote this goal of her party. It appears that she silently works and stands by the principles that her dear family dedicated itself to.

Sonia Gandhi's entire façade, as I witnessed during my appointment with her, simply tempted my mind and heart to reflect. I *wish to meet her again.* I expressed a desire to meet her in her residence at 10 Janpath, New Delhi. Again and again, I discovered in my research the power in this person to pursue her goals against all odds, to work for the betterment of the larger good of the society. I found this fabulously tempting. Matching her cool way of function, I felt comfortable and ecstatic to have been accommodated with an appointment with Sonia Gandhi, something that a commoner like me would find almost impossible with any such celebrity in any similar situation. In real life, during our meeting, she simply lived up to the personality I had imagined after I had thoroughly enjoyed the process of inspiring myself by reading so many books before I met her. Sonia Gandhi can certainly be a role model, and this is my firm belief. All the descriptions of the greatness in Sonia Gandhi that I had meticulously read about seemed to take life in this appointment. It was a truly remarkable experience!

I felt as if I was in seventh heaven all day after I met her. Indeed, I seemed unable to recover from that appointment. Sonia Gandhi is among the most misunderstood public figures today. She is a politician who has worked hard behind the scenes, so to speak, for generations' worth, and yet not many people outside the political circles know enough about her to appreciate this hard work. I did not think I wished to recover from our meeting; I was undoubtedly euphoric.

A critical review of the blue ink asks why is there no mention of the content of my conversation with Sonia Gandhi? It would have made my book more worthy

My view is it is a hard task to present to compress everything in one part of the book

Like as I said at the cost of repetition it is an one woman one show multitasking every role that made this book I invite traditional publishers to hereby support

I received a writers feedback in Malayalam Language (Indian state Kerala has official state language Malayalam) asking me to write a book in Malayalam for Kerala Malayalam speaking population I respectfully hereby invite Kerala authors to feel free to get in touch with me via email roopabedigere7@gmail.com so we can progress this idea

As I came out of the Parliament House in New Delhi, I met a few striking personalities. Prominent amongst them was Chiranjeevi, the popular Telugu actor and member of Parliament. I shook hands with him and said, 'Lovely work, sir.'

Now Chiranjeevi Sir made a guest entry into Indian politics and he spoke a few sentences to me in Telugu (I sincerely wish I could speak and talk in all languages of the world ....!) Then he spoke in Hindi and a little of English inviting me to discuss Unfortunately that again failed to take shape This is my response to Chiranjeevi Sir and all the lovely Telugu speaking people please feel free to get in touch via my email roopabedigere7@gmail.com we can progress your thoughts if they are not yet outdated I like to believe, social media and technology can create magic and am pleased with your thoughts sir and lovely work once again

For the non Indian English speaking reader Chiranjeevi Sir is a Famous India Cinema star with great following in South India and the telugu speaking population of the US and the UK and elsewhere

I also met Ambika Soni, the former union minister in India. She kindly accommodated my greeting, and I said, 'Madam, I wish to write a book on Sonia Gandhi.' She said, 'Please do.' It was a simply courteous gesture that the former minister perhaps expressed. She continues her work into Congress party

As I stood in the corridors of the Parliament, I watched some powerful politicians of the previous governments. I recognized some of them, and some gentleman workers there helped me identify others. I was escorted safely out of the Parliament, where I had been for easily a good few hours.One gentleman suggested I meet Jaylalitha madam (sadly she is no more at the time of this publication)Jayalaitha madam is yet another powerful Indian politician from the south of India speaking mainly Tamil(Tamil is the most widely spoken language in the state of Tamilnadu in South India)

Phew! My mind had so much information and so many pictures to digest, yet the lovely feeling of the smiling Sonia Gandhi seemed to linger on. This visit was something that left an indelible impression on my mind. It was not just a simple smile. It was the vast difference she had made via the policies in the Congress party that I had read about and researched continuously while sitting in the London Library. The policies that Congress supported over decades under Sonia Gandhi's presidency were issues that I had followed closely while in India and even after I moved to England. As an observer I can easily match my impression of Sonia Gandhi with the powerful positive side of her that I think is easy to not miss.I welcome readers to write to me if anything has chosen to miss.

I felt it was great that I had met Sonia Gandhi.

Now that I was in the power capital, New Delhi, I wished to make some more efforts to help my understanding. I now worked continuously and decided to attend a session in Parliament. I made a rather strenuous attempt to see a parliamentary session. I came to understand that the public are allowed into the public gallery. As I stepped onto the green-carpeted huge hall, I felt it certainly looked brighter than Westminster in London. I was just stunned at the huge hall, and said *wow* to myself. There is an innermost hall where current government members and opposition members meet. It was under tight security, and staff members led us, the general public, into the building. I was pleased to be able to choose a seat for myself from which I could see Sonia Gandhi best. I sat with her directly opposite me, simply to observe her closely. I did not talk, and I was not overcome by emotion. I just sat there observing Sonia Gandhi mostly, along with many other leaders from the ruling party. This gave me a lovely opportunity to observe her at close quarters, which enabled me to learn more about her style of functioning at work. This was exactly what I wished to highlight in this book. There was an assigned section for the journalists just adjacent to the public gallery.

I found Sonia Gandhi in the front seat with two other senior leaders from the opposition, one on either side of her. My initial view was that Sonia Gandhi is a star politician; she was absolutely fascinating. This was the first time I witnessed Sonia Gandhi at work. I saw some serious political business in full action, and sat in the opposition. Sonia Gandhi was dressed in an exquisitely handcrafted, hand loomed, beautiful white sari with a black border. She also wore a saffron thread on her right wrist. (It is my understanding that most devout Hindus wear this.) Her traditional Indian costume with black heels was unforgettable. She was impeccably dressed in her well-known signature costume.

Sonia Gandhi was clearly aware of the proceedings, especially from the opposition, and every debate that found its place in the Parliament that I found striking in the entire Parliament session I intently observed in one entire session.

The reason I noted this was that it was easy to spot some members listening only when either their turn to present arrived, or they were the focus of the topic discussed – especially if that topic met their liking. I witnessed her conversing with the other leaders in a quiet whisper. Sonia Gandhi, I found, was an adept observer in the sense that she appeared to make note of every act in the Parliament. This led me to appreciate this remarkable skill that perhaps had been nurtured by Sonia Gandhi for decades. The perfection I saw in Sonia Gandhi in this assembly was something of a brilliance. I sat there speculating how much her vast experience of this kind, spanning for more than two decades, must have accrued, and how it must help her in her hard work. Surely this is reflected in the phenomenal political decisions that have emerged out of her presidency of the Congress or its alliance. In some respects, surviving the difficult decisions single-handedly is no small achievement, and it has all been for the betterment of the use of politics. I have no hesitation in stating this certainly deserves due respect. Without a doubt, such a person who deserves all such accolades and respect is Sonia Gandhi. I have watched the current Congress leader Priyanka Gandhi in sessions online and I can see replicas of her mother's ways of functioning always making notes and observations and occupying strategic positions too

I prized the poise and grace Sonia Gandhi displayed when, on several occasions, she walked gracefully out in a perfectly innocuous manner and bowed to the acting speaker. Yes, I did see a lot of the façade of the late Mrs Indira Gandhi on this occasion in the Parliament House. Many others have already remarked about this; however, it is my view that Sonia Gandhi is unique … unique indeed.

Subjects of national and international interest were discussed during this hour that I witnessed. As our allotted time in the public viewing gallery came to an end, we were led to the outside. There was a gallery section limited to the press. This was to facilitate the next group of people coming in to attend the public gallery. Before I could imagine anything, I was out of the Parliament House. As I made my way out, I noted members of the press outside. They were busy interviewing people. As members of the public, we were restrained from taking part in any of these sessions. As I made my way out, the crowd waiting to attend the next available session seemed to never diminish.

Being a doctor and constantly aware of health and safety issues, I noted one thing predominantly: should there occur a health issue for any of the public viewers or even the politicians there in and around the Parliament House security zone, this looked like a danger zone to me. There was no easy access for ambulance or emergency services. There were no in-house doctor services in the Parliament! I earnestly hope this changes in the time to come. Yes Changes have happened indeed a new Parliament house 2023 has been built and I hope it has services for medical and the special abled can access special provisions for access at the time

It was a short journey and a short stay in New Delhi that I made specifically to visit Sonia Gandhi. After I finished my two special occasions of observing Sonia Gandhi, I wished to seize another wishful opportunity to meet her. This time I made attempts to contact the official sources at 10 Janpath, New Delhi, which I believe is the official residence of Sonia Gandhi. There is a dedicated team at 10 Janpath. The staff kindly accommodated my request and told me they would offer an appointment over the next few days if possible. Being a mother of two young boys, I knew that my family commitments and professional commitments simply did not provide me the flexibility to prolong my stay in New Delhi however much I wished to. The officials at 10 Janpath did not seem to want to endorse my book either, as I seemed to get this message clearly as expected.

This book is purely the result of my determination to inspire myself as much as many other people, especially women, who are being discriminated against. I want them to know what it means to fight together for a universal common cause of spreading peace, harmony, tolerance, and freedom. My son, Skanda Venkatesh, who then was eight years old, is aware of Sonia Gandhi as a celebrity from India. At the time he was in grade four doing his studies in one of the schools in England. He asked me for a promise – I should tell him if I had a cup of tea with Sonia Gandhi. As I caught my Emirates Airline flight in New Delhi to return to Manchester, I sat in my seat thinking, *I will have to disappoint my son as I did not get a chance to have tea with Sonia Gandhi.* But, as the old English saying goes, I told myself, *Never say never.* Skanda's eyes lit up as he heard me talk with him on the phone before my return home about Sonia Gandhi. He said, 'Mummy, I want you to tell me the whole experience as best as you can when you return.' I thought, *I'll be unable to detail every single thought. I shall simply ask my son to wait to read the book himself!*

That was the first time I had been in the New Delhi Airport. I found it to be one of the finest modern airports. I was all by myself. I read a few interesting books and sincerely hoped that my own book would find itself on those shelves. My book on Sonia Gandhi – *Sonia Gandhi The Power Part 1*, by Roopa Venktesh, should be a must read for anyone who would like to be inspired by the story of Sonia Gandhi. This is the silent wishful thinking that echoed in my heart.

Why should this book showcase Sonia Gandhi better? The answer is that perhaps I am one of the few women writers who can echo the right sentiments. This is my view. I am a woman writer who perhaps can appreciate the odds that Sonia Gandhi has undergone in strengthening, growing, and nurturing the ideas of the Congress. (Please note wherever I mention Congress I refer to the Indian National Congress, the main political party in India, or any such alliance that the Congress led by Sonia Gandhi supports, like the United Progressive Alliance, popularly known as UPA.) There should be no barrier to prevent the achievement of the legitimate goals of the good purpose of human life. Yet, over time, we in human society have adopted and been given characteristics that appear to not be protected, like gender, age, nationality, race, community, religion, language, and numerous such unknown variables.

It is amazing, indeed, that in a struggling world full of already present difficulties that cannot be conquered, such as natural disasters like floods and earthquakes, these distinguishing characteristics seem to assume enough importance to bar people from attaining fairness in society. Overall, this blocks personal and societal development and progress of every society and the whole world.

In simple terms, any woman achiever in modern times has to have surpassed many odds and deserves considerable support and respect.

I began to work on what the title of the book should be, having seen the titles of the many books already written about Sonia Gandhi. The striking title that I thought befitted Sonia Gandhi was 'The Power'. Here I did not mean the power of the office metaphorically. I meant it as an antithesis, as she is a real politician who works for the power of policies that can help humanity rather than the power of the office or position. I referred to Sonia Gandhi's power of success in the office of the presidency of Congress influencing the governments without actually being in a race for power. I meant the power of sacrifice of her dear husband, Rajiv Gandhi, and her dear mother-in-law, Indira Gandhi, that Sonia Gandhi endured.

Sonia Gandhi holds the power of the faith of Congress to give back the power to the underprivileged classes by empowering them with policies that target their needs, and perhaps to the rest of the electorate who have had faith in congress ideals. She is a politician who is noteworthy – a politician who gives back the power to the people by empowering them via policies. My sole carefully observed view is that she is a true politician.

Sonia Gandhi uses her power to fight against all odds for the betterment of all communities and the larger good of society. The power and resilience in Sonia Gandhi I hope shall touch the chord of struggling underprivileged people in Indian society(Though middle class inched the lower class still remains a majority and the real India and INC is the only party championing their cause through the decades consistently). She has the power to stand up for the grossly neglected, yet a significantly major, farming population. India has one of the highest number of people living below the poverty line in the world or should I say these underprivileged can be uplifted they shall be a huge national and international human resource. During Sonia Gandhi's presidency, there has always been a powerful emphasis on such an underprivileged class such as the farmers. She fights for their autonomy and their best interests. Sonia Gandhi's presidency ensured the strengthening of many useful policies, such as the Common Minimum Programme set up by Rajiv Gandhi. Sonia Gandhi's power of interest in reviving the policies and regulations and central programmes, started by Rajiv Gandhi's attempt to address the needs of the underprivileged sections, is historic. No doubt there is more to be done. Would hatred amongst communities grow the development? There is such hatred and lack of protection related to human values based on characteristics like gender, age, nationality, community, race, and language. The list seems endless, and is, without a doubt, detrimental to any development or progress of society and a country at large.

With globalization affecting all sectors as it never has before, it is amazing that discrimination carries on, silently affecting growth, development, and fairness in a destructive way.

Dear readers, I welcome every one of you to reflect on how to *stop* or at least begin to stop these feelings of hatred or discrimination based on characteristics that are unwanted in our humanity. This must start somewhere. I plead with every reader reading this book to actively discourage such thoughts and actions, and to work for a common cause. Appreciate women achievers like Sonia Gandhi, who protect such variables. My sincere plea is to at least fight for a common good cause – the larger good for all communities.

While discriminating against a person based on gender or nationality, what we are failing to understand is that we are blocking our own development and betterment. Discrimination crushes the individual and does no good for the majority, even those who are not discriminated against. Imagine this happening on a large scale. The result may be as bad as a civil unrest, lack of development, and war – a colossal waste of resources and a source of bloodshed. I join my dear readers in reflection. Do we really need this in this world? This thought I am certain is dormant in every reader – that we could live happily without discrimination, hatred, and killings. I first wrote this book in 2015, the world now in 2025 is witnessing wars in Russia,Ukraine and Israel and Palestine(with new entrants like Iran Syria!) since last few years

I invite every reader to appreciate a famous Sanskrit philosophy Vasudai*va kutumbakam*. This literally means that the world is a family, and so it is time we reflect on our own to see what we have done or what we are doing in terms of working within the family. We have been amidst hatred for our own family – I mean the world. Simply put, a leader politician like Sonia Gandhi has to sincerely plead nationally on national television in a democracy like India to inspire people to stop hating others based on communities, religion, and so forth. Such hatred is appalling indeed. This widespread hatred does not seem to stop in developed countries either, and as a matter of fact, victimizes our own brothers and sisters, and still worse, children and those yet to be born! It is a very ugly ongoing reality. Do we need this? People worldwide experience violence as a result of gaining power to trade, vandalism, communal conflicts (still ongoing at the time of writing this book in many parts of the world), border disputes, and civil racist actions. They all continue to take their toll. Many resources are lost under these circumstances of hatred, discrimination, and war. We could use resources(wasted into antisocial wars etc) elsewhere; for example, in regions like Africa and Asia where people die of starvation and thirst. We could wipe out poverty and make the world a better place for our own families. We must not forget the hidden poverty in developed nations either.

Why do I bring up this topic of hatred and discrimination based on gender here? Because many great politicians and great souls would probably have not been killed except for this discrimination, as an extreme form of hatred has resulted in assassinations. (The most recent comment is worth reflecting where leader Donald Trump's own words state 'Deepseated hatred is crazily existing Ref you tube video https://www.youtube.com/watch?v=oZTupX3809s) These politicians we have lost could have turned this world into a better place. Politicians like Sonia Gandhi who work for nonviolence are opposed; they do not seem to be supported, even though their efforts are for such a common good cause. It is time we reflect on these moral values, as it is these moral values that differentiate us, as human beings, from animals.

I like to also strongly condemn the acts of attempts to shoot Donald J Trump,the current respectful president in everyway two times !. Its ok to respectfully disagree, place arguments but attacking someone violently is sad and sad that it is continuing in the form of wars etc and I hate to believe it may until we can all join in and raise a unified voice to stop and it is completely stoppable.

Sonia Gandhi was born in Orbassano, twelve miles from Turin in Italy on December 9, 1946. The wide references I have referred to suggest that she was a very naughty, very active child, although good at her studies. One of the references referred to Sonia Gandhi's childhood qualities as a young girl as intelligent, charming, and very hardworking. The grassroots of Sonia Gandhi's childhood intelligence, hard work, and charm are easily recognized in her career in politics. Sonia Gandhi was born to a conservative, staunchly Roman Catholic, traditional Italian family. As a young girl, she wanted to be a teacher. I can see qualities in her that would make her a good teacher.

Even as a politician, she advocates to stop hatred against others based on religion, community, gender, language, and so on.

Sonia Gandhi sheds tears for her family. The tears probably say, 'I have worked hard to live up to your fight for the Congress. I wish you were with me so then these tears would become my tears of joy! Congress president Sonia Gandhi after paying tribute to Indira Gandhi on her 95th birth anniversary on Nov 19 2012 in New Delhi'.

My heartfelt view is, do we need to hate people? Do we have to hate because someone is a woman, because someone belongs to a different nationality, or because someone cannot speak a particular language or because whatever ? In my view, any idea for society must be considered by protecting the characteristics of a person, and in Sonia Gandhi's case, her gender and nationality must be protected, as well as all her ideals of the Congress party that she works for with respect, for decades. She should be considered and respected for this. As a matter of fact, the Congress was originated by a foreigner. A. O. Hulme was the pioneer of the historic longest-ever active party, Indian National Congress in modern-day politics in world history. Although the Congress that originated before India gained independence has transformed to the Congress Party of today, it is perhaps interesting that the needless opposition that Sonia Gandhi has to face is uniquely targeted at her. Personally I have faced a lot of disrespect in my profession and personal life 'because I am a woman because..sometimes I sadly cannot come to terms with any unfair possible reason other than the fact that I am a woman !

Just to reflect on some historic facts: Many inventions and discoveries of the world would not make our society richer if the society had discriminated against such persons on the basis of gender, nationality, language, and religion. The Swedish-based Nobel Committee might not consider people from a particular nation to carry the message of peace if they were prejudiced. This prize is open to the entire world, and so should be the basis of any ideal in any society.

I like to bring in the facts of ancient India, India is the home to the largest number of social reformers and religious thinkers from Sanathan Dharma(The religion known as Hindu to the anglophone countries)India never invaded any other country and India is the most benevolent country accommodating all religious faiths more communally than any other nation across the world I hope the futuristic media technologies can unearth our ancient rich culture tradition and history of India and her ancient civilization An average Indian is a law abiding and resourceful Sanathan Dharma follower (I don't think an average anglophone reader can appreciate this paragraph but this is to emphasise non hatred and humane spiritual principles upholding the universal peace originates here probably is my view)

Sonia Gandhi lived in England in the early '60s at around the same time Rajiv Gandhi, the son of Indira Gandhi, came to live in England. Rajiv met Sonia in 1965. According to one reference I read, Rajiv had striking looks, was reserved and gentle, had big black eyes and a wonderfully innocent and disarming smile. Sonia is said to have described Rajiv saying, 'There was not a trace of cunning in Rajiv.'

Sonia and Rajiv's love at first sight culminated in a fairytale wedding. There have been no references to suggest that Sonia Gandhi was after the position that Rajiv was likely to have after their wedding. It is also clear that Sonia Gandhi wedded herself completely to the subcontinent by this precious relationship between herself and the handsome Shri Rajiv Gandhi. There seems there was no thought in Sonia Gandhi whatsoever of the future memorable career in serving the Congress party for more than two decades at this historical point.

One reference describes how Shri Rajiv Gandhi met Sonia Gandhi in 1965 in England in Cambridgeshire. One warm English evening the couple were are believed to have met in a Greek restaurant in Cambridgeshire. They got to know each other through a common friend. Rajiv Gandhi was described as having striking looks, big black eyes and wonderfully innocent and disarming smile. Sonia Gandhi is said to have found incredible security in Rajiv Gandhi. Sonia Gandhi was Rajiv Gandhi's first and only girlfriend. Rajiv Gandhi initially spent some time in Cambridgeshire. He joined Imperial College of Science and Technology and stayed for less than a year. In an official interview, Rajiv Gandhi is said to say that when he first saw and met Sonia, something in him seemed to confirm that 'this shall be the person I wish to have in my life.'

In fact, after Sonia's marriage there are references that indicate that she was never keen that Rajiv pursue any active role in politics. The reason she was clear about this was that it would mean a compromise in family life in some respects. However, from within political and non- political circles, expectations of this family of Gandhi rode high. Everyone would naturally view this couple as future dynastic leaders. One of the references about Sonia Gandhi stated that she was only about five foot five inches tall and, like Jacqueline Kennedy, shunned the press.

There seems no evidence that Sonia Gandhi ever faced a barrier of nationality, language, or culture when she married. Love and unflinching commitment overcame all barriers to an everlasting relationship as she committed herself to her precious relationship with Rajiv Gandhi and his family. If this meant a lot of changes, it seems she welcomed them into her life. Sonia Gandhi declared in an official interview that it was not easy to adjust to this totally different Indian culture, which was so different from her origins. She declared that her love for Rajiv Gandhi made all such difficulties not turn into barriers as she allowed herself to become steeped into the Indian Culture. What is commendable is that Sonia Gandhi continues to transform her life after the tragic demise of her dear husband.

How then, did the helpless Sonia Gandhi face the fact that her dear husband, Rajiv Gandhi, was ripped apart in a brutal assassination by a suicide bomber? It must have been heartbreaking indeed. The beautiful, charming, and handsome husband, Rajiv Gandhi, was barely cognisable after the bomb exploded. Even to imagine this is absolutely shocking indeed. How would Sonia Gandhi survive to live strongly with such painful memories of this? She is finding a respite by carrying the torch of the Congress party, which certainly reminds Sonia Gandhi of what her husband held dear. Rajiv Gandhi's death certainly was not a fairytale ending to their story that anyone would have expected. And certainly they would not have expected Sonia

Gandhi to forge ahead and soldier on. This is a drama that one can barely even visualise. Yet this is a political story of sorts in the history of modern contemporary politics.

One of the references quotes: 'Recounted in Sonia's simple prose it's a story of remarkable endurance, courage, and resolve.' This reflects how a shy provincial girl who was so terrified of meeting her prospective mother-in-law for the first time could change history in a foreign land. Sonia Gandhi has done that three times. The first was 1998 when she took over a Congress that was threatening to implode and nursed it back to life and victory in sixteen states. Second when she supports her children into politics Third she continues dynamically in different roles

Surely the charisma of a foreign-born person, Sonia Gandhi, lies in her innate decisions that made India her home. It is her work for Indians that has made her career. She risks death and dishonour from undignified remarks from misplaced interests. To say that Sonia Gandhi depends on the charisma of her dynastic family is incorrect. Sonia Gandhi's long hiatus of six years completely led the masses to forget the trauma and emotional pains she must have endured. There is no report of the Congress either supporting her during this period, barring the repeated requests from party leaders to accept the presidency. It is also incorrect to label Sonia Gandhi's victory in 2004 as largely 'a sympathy vote' for the reviving widow. Even though the Indian contains a significant number of illiterates, the decision to vote for Sonia Gandhi is a clear mandate that one must not forget. The electorate decided to place their faith in Sonia Gandhi, as they were familiar with the rule of former members of the Gandhi

The legacy of the Congress has been nurtured the most despite some stunning comebacks and deepsetbacks

To say that Sonia Gandhi depends on the charisma of her dynastic family is incorrect. Sonia Gandhi's long hiatus of six years completely led the masses to forget the trauma and emotional pains she must have endured. There is no report of the Congress either supporting her during this period, barring the repeated requests from party leaders to accept the presidency. It is also incorrect to label Sonia Gandhi's victory in 2004 as largely 'a sympathy vote' for the reviving widow. Even though the Indian contains a significant number of illiterates, the decision to vote for Sonia Gandhi is a clear mandate that one must not forget. The electorate decided to place their faith in Sonia Gandhi, as they were familiar with the rule of former members of the Gandhi

The electorate decided to place their faith in Sonia Gandhi, as they were familiar with the rule of former members of the Gandhi family. Even so, it is incorrect to suggest that Sonia Gandhi won the elections because of the name Gandhi. The Gandhi- Nehru household knows how to rule, and this was clear to the Indian electorate. The governance machinery augured by the Congress is something that can barely be deciphered by any other party in India. The Congress-led governance is a carefully planned policy with substantial long-term results that often are easy to miss.

After Sonia Gandhi's advent, this government underwent a dynamic transformation to meet the challenges of the needs of the electorate, and this is the key to the success of Sonia Gandhi that one can barely understand let alone appreciate. She has achieved astounding results, and there will be more in the years to come.

Sonia Gandhi's view on emergency: The Indira Gandhi I knew was a democrat at heart to the core and, although circumstances compelled her to take that action, she was never comfortable with it.

Excerpts from one of Sonia Gandhi's speeches:

I fought like a tigress for him, for us, and for our children, and for the life we made together on Rajiv joining politics. When I married and joined Indira Gandhi's household, I was welcomed with open arms.

Through them I was also accepted by the country. Today I consider myself a daughter of mother India. The remains of my husband lie in this land. And till the day I die, this will also be my land. For me that [becoming PM] is not a priority. My priority is to defeat this government. Let's see when the time comes.

Sonia Gandhi is regarded as one of the world's most private leaders, and perhaps will be a revered leader ever to accept a foreign country as her own and

Ten Janpath has assumed greater importance than ever before thanks to Sonia Gandhi's renunciation of the position of prime minister in 2004. While the other members of the Gandhi family assumed importance after occupying that office, Sonia Gandhi is unique in renouncing the office and assumming importance out of position or chair. It shall remain the most powerful political decision ever in the history of contemporary politics. The world should never failed to recognise this. Ten Janpath, the official address of Sonia Gandhi, is considered one of the most powerful addresses, more powerful than 7 Racecourse, New Delhi, the official residence of the prime minister of India. Every foreign dignitary likes to give a courtesy call at 10 Janpath.

Sonia Gandhi holds honorary doctorates from the University of Madras and Brussels University, and the Order of King Leopold from the government of Belgium.

Sonia Gandhi's stated, 'The Congress party has won and lost many elections. In victory or defeat, we must remember that it is our solemn duty to serve people to the best of our ability.'

Sonia Gandhi has faced some health issues. In 2011, she underwent surgery in the United States for an undisclosed medical condition. In 2014, she was rushed to a hospital from the parliament looking ill and unsteady. Her dedication to the job made all these medical issues history.

She officially took charge of the Congress party in 1998 and was elected to Parliament in 1999.

Sonia Gandhi herself said in a television interview, 'I never felt they look at me as a foreigner because I'm not. I am Indian.'

Sonia Gandhi spent the seventies steeped in Indian Culture. In 1984, Indira Gandhi was assassinated by her Sikh bodyguards in retaliation for her decision to send troops into their holiest shrine, the Golden Temple.

In August 2000, Sonia Gandhi became a grandmother for the first time when her daughter, Priyanka, gave birth to a son.

Sonia Gandhi is a familiar figure in Amethi, her husband's rural parliamentary constituency in the northern state of Uttar Pradesh, which her son, Rahul Gandhi, also has held representation of. She herself has represented the neighbouring seat of Rai Bareilly in Uttar Pradesh

One of the references wrote, 'By refusing the prime minister's chair, Mrs. Sonia Gandhi has shown the nation that she is the true successor of the Nehru-Gandhi dynasty and that she has acquired the spirit of patriotism of which her father-in- law, Feroz Gandhi, and her grandfather-in-law, Pt. Jawaharlal Lal Nehru both are outstanding examples in the history of freedom movement of India. The impact of this silent revolution can be easily seen.'

Sonia Gandhi has proved beyond all doubts that one does not become Indian solely by birth. Indianness can be earned and acquired by following Indian culture and traditions. It requires love and selfless commitment and the strength of will to put the interest of the country above one's own. Sonia Gandhi's renunciation and self-denial has left the opposition without any agenda. Her unprecedented move has touched India, and more so Hindu India, at a much deeper level because the ideals of selflessness and renunciation that guided her action are embedded in the core of Hindu religion. Here I have to mention that one need not kill another to prove a point and truly the sanathan culture that invents principles of humanity is the best that India has to offer to the whole world I am a Hindu by faith by practice and by birth

Fortunately for me I am a doctor who by taking an oath treat everyone as equal, lives suffering or dying I see no difference naturally in my view of a association of every non Hindu I take pride in saying I am the only one I can remember never nurturing every single person group caste or religion,race in my wonderful amazing journey of training(in medicine) and healing poeple To me my life as a student was everyone as a family everyone as I became a doctor I embraced the whole

To me my life as a student was everyone as a family everyone as I became a doctor I embraced the whole world as a family true to the core of the religion I practice and follow I have to mention some amazing people who nurtured my professional and personal development include Hindu,Christians,British,Americans(and other religions too) and people worldwide I feel fortunate to have recieved a written acknowledgement from Prince Harry.The Duke of Sussex

As a Indian Dr I served Indians and immigrants here and as a British Dr I served the lovely British people in the UK I sincerely and seriously have no time to think how people have time to hate something while there is hardly anytime to enjoy respect,grow and prosper with the beautiful things that the world has potentially to offer

Sonia Gandhi became the president of All India Congress. Incidentally, she was the fifth from the Nehru family to do so, the other four being Moti Lal Nehru, Jawhar Lal Nehru, Indira Gandhi, and Rajeev Gandhi. In no time Sonia Gandhi was elevated as dual chief of the Indian National Congress party and its parliamentary party and thus emulated her husband, her mother-in-law, grandfather-in-law – Rajeev, Indira, and Nehru – who all held the two posts during their careers.

A senior congress leader said Sonia Gandhi, is totally, round-the-clock, passionately involved in party affairs and one should not underestimate her hardwork.

Sonia Gandhi carried forward MNREGA, Right to Education, Food Security Law, and Land Acquisition Law amongst others.

Through its first term in office, Sonia Gandhi supported UPA government passed several landmark bills aimed at social reform. These included an employment guarantee bill, the Right to Information Act, and a right to education act.

'Amazing Grace' was the headline verdict of the *Hindustan Times* when Sonia Gandhi renounced the office of prime minister. Most of the newspapers reported that, by declining the prime minister's post, Sonia Gandhi had taken the high moral ground and put her rivals on the back foot.

For one, it allowed her to assume the high moral ground and signal that she was by no means enamoured of power for its own sake, but power for the principles she believes in.

'She has thus neatly disarmed her political opponents of the one weapon they had hoped to use against her.'

She was a reluctant politician. She was in it out of a sense of duty, not because of ambition,' wrote Analyst Vir Sanghvi, *Hindustan Times.*

Just as Sonia Gandhi's great love for Rajiv Gandhi never recognized that they were of totally different races, cultures, religions, and languages amongst other variables, Sonia Gandhi's style of functioning in the Congress as a president sees no discrimination against any congressman or congresswoman due to such variables.

This is something I have noted avidly in Sonia Gandhi's style of functioning.

Sonia Gandhi earnestly listens to every word of her supporters from any state, caste, community, religion, and language. She never fails to listen to the supporters of Congress. This is what defines her classic success in her Congress presidency. Every voice is heard in Sonia Gandhi's framework of politics. Congress President Sonia Gandhi meets farmers in Haryana asking government to provide compensation to farmers 2015.

Sonia Gandhi not only welcomed Rajiv Gandhi and his family into her heart, she welcomed the ideals of Congress that her family, in Rajiv Gandhi and Indira Gandhi, had established. It appears that she little realized she would herself have to carry their roles alone in time to come.

On 25 January 1968, Rajiv and Sonia Gandhi got engaged. On 25 February 1968, on Basant Panchami, an an auspicious day for Hindus and also the same day that Indira Gandhi is said to have got married, Rajiv Gandhi and the young and beautiful Sonia were married at six in the evening at One Safdurjung Road. The beautiful Sonia wore a pink sari that was given to her by her mother-in-law, Indira Gandhi (who apparently had worn the same pink sari for her wedding. A shloka, or song, from The Rigveda, an ancient Indian collection of Vedic

Sanskrit hymns, was sung during the Jaimala ceremony. Jaimala is a Hindu ritual that is practised during the wedding ceremony, in which the bride and bridegroom exchange custom-made flower garlands, which are worn around the neck.

Sonia Gandhi has always been known as a remarkably non-controversial persona, and it is perhaps in her nature, from her subconscious, not to harbour any ill feelings or hatred to anyone on any basis whatsoever. Some of the references describing Sonia Gandhi explain that she is a gentle person in her manners.

In my only ever dream appointment with Sonia Gandhi in April 2015, I noticed this natural trait in her – the particular tenderness in her as a mother, grandmother, and wife who had endured many hardships and sacrifices. As a responsible Congress president, Sonia Gandhi's gentle nature has helped her be poised in successes as well as during setbacks, allowing her the flexibility to deal with people. She has brought great moderation to the party.

Sonia Gandhi is a connoisseur of art and has a good eye for antiques and Indian handicrafts and hand-loomed fabrics. She has a special interest in Indian contemporary classical and tribal art.

Sonia Gandhi's favourite pastime is reading, and some other, more indiscrete, references say shopping is another inconsistent hobby. She completed an art restoration course from the National Gallery of Modern Art.

In 1983 Sonia Gandhi renounced her Italian citizenship.

On 26 June 1975, emergency was declared in India during the rule of Indira Gandhi. The emergency days saw some of the toughest political and civil unrest movements in India, which challenged Indira Gandhi's prowess.

After the tragic assassination of Indira Gandhi, Rajiv Gandhi became the youngest prime minister in India's history at the age of forty. Sonia Gandhi consented to this move of the 'family' with a heavy heart, it appeared, and in one official interview, Rajiv Gandhi explained that he had explained to his wife that the turn of events had been inevitable, to which Sonia Gandhi is said to have gently agreed. When Rajiv Gandhi asked the consent of Sonia Gandhi to accept the office of prime minister, she said she was worried that her husband might be killed; however, Rajiv Gandhi said that he might be killed even if he didn't accept the position. This is the resolve of the Nehru-Gandhi family. It appears that the family is 'prepared' to sacrifice, as if it is the family affair.

Sonia Gandhi was a hostess mostly while Rajiv Gandhi was the prime minister, and there are no references to ever suggest any inkling of her participation in politics. Rajiv Gandhi is said to have stated, 'Sonia Gandhi was always a person who would not like to be in the spotlight or pose in the public. Sonia Gandhi was a generally shy person. Sonia Gandhi always had much-needed empathy for the disabled sections of the society. This is something that Sonia Gandhi's party actively promotes – emphasis on the less-empowered sections of society. It is perhaps correct to say that Sonia Gandhi retains the part of her personality that is not keen on marketing or wanting to be in spotlight, yet the Congress president is no more someone who wishes not be in public. Sonia Gandhi, in her first-ever campaign in the late nineties when she took charge as the president of the Congress party, travelled over 63,000 kilometres and addressed more than sixty large public meetings across the breadth and length of the subcontinent.

Rajiv Gandhi's tenure as a prime minister and congress president was short lived following his tragic assassination that did not provide a happy fairytale ending for Sonia Gandhi's married life.

Imagine the turmoil in Sonia Gandhi's heart and mind after this tragic event. The thought sends shivers along the spine of any woman.

She had placed all her faith, trust, and life on her love for her dear husband, Rajiv Gandhi. She had made a foreign country her own and was forced to see her husband sacrificed, actually ripped apart to be no more recognizable. That must have been heartbreaking! Her dear mother-in-law, Indira Gandhi, was no more, and now her soul mate and her dear husband, Rajiv Gandhi, was no more. How did she survive this shock and live through the first moments without her ever- loving husband?

Sonia Gandhi actually survived that shocking period to eventually step into Rajiv Gandhi's shoes as a president of Congress. Certainly such a decision was not simple. It was a decision that rode the spirit of Congress high enough to gain a victory in the oncoming general elections. It simply did not mean that Sonia Gandhi gained sympathy votes. That is an incorrect observation in my view. The presence, hard work, and dedication of Sonia Gandhi in her role of president helped Congress

The steel in Sonia Gandhi carried her along as she looked after her children, Priyanka and Rahul. Sonia Gandhi, it appeared, stayed away from politics, and despite numerous requests for her to enter the political arena, she seemed reluctant. In my view they have observed politics from far and so they are passively always involved

It has been said that Sonia Gandhi's daughter, Priyanka, was offered a position in the Congress party when she was barely twenty-five years old. She now makes the expected comeback and plays dynamic roles in the party well buttressed by brother

Rahul Gandhi Both Priyanka Gandhi and Rahul Gandhi shoulder dynamic roles in Congress party and they follow the same time tested principles in gluing the effective output.Yes there is some glaring truth in this whole scheme They make strategic decisions and they expect the same from every congress leader and congress supporter switching roles is a day to day affair as though a potential Prime minister could be the president of a the Indian national Congress and a potential Congress leader Kishorilal Sharma sir could fight an election Sonia Gandhi became the All India Congress Committee member in 1998.

Sonia Gandhi had shared a good bond with Indira Gandhi, and despite not being keen on politics, she must have felt an obligation to accept that the family continue to work for Congress. If that meant the sacrifice of lives, then the heavy- hearted Sonia Gandhi had to make some life-changing decisions. Foremost amongst the decisions was consenting to Rajiv accepting the office of prime minister. Rajiv Gandhi explained in a candid televised interview that he had to 'convince' Sonia that he had to accept the office of prime minister and that Sonia understood. The second important decision was herself stepping into Rajiv Gandhi's shoes as a president of Congress.

Sonia Gandhi is fluent in Hindi, English, French, Spanish, Italian, and Russian. There are around thousands of dialects in India and around 22 officially recognised languages spoken in India, and one may easily find two Indians understanding each other in the English language better than they would in their original Indian dialects. English links Indians best to the world, both outside and inside India. The English language also provides the best link between the northern and southern parts of India.

India was colonized by the British, and English was the language with which the British government governed India in the pre-independence times, before 1947. English continues to be used in

Indian governance, with English sharing same status as Hindi, which is the national language. In fact, due to the enormous list of hundreds of dialects and languages with a long list of cultures and subcultures within the subcontinent, English seems to be more prominent and 'national' in many respects. With globalization and English fluency fetching more jobs from outside of India and the anglo phone countries, English is preferred and in a increasingly global world I encourage multilanguage ability and I dont mind learning Chinese,Russian and Japanese languages or any language that can connect us and prosper us absolutely

In fact, in many cultured communities within India and perhaps amongst Indians abroad, a good command of a foreign language – English or French – gains higher status perhaps because of the connectivity to the global language and culture, and more importantly globalization. The Indian diaspora is successful outside India due to a good command of English, the global language that connects more of us.There are around close to 40 million Indians outside of India I call upon Indian government to facilitate more easy emigration of talented India to outside of India, and I live to believe this as no brain drain It infact diversifies the systems Equally I call upon the developed countries of the US,UK,Australia,Singapore and others accord and facilitate easy job and development for each of the nations and of the world I think there need be global thinking in everything It appears idiotic to me to travel to for e.g South Africa to get a chinese apple for say 50 pounds worth to gain.0007 percent GDP of some measure That is a jargon present to say for eg.Raghuram rajan sir who may unravel clearly in economy language what globalisation can mean stopping wars etc can mean to humanity we as the whole have got to think better act better and achieve better and better I invite all interested readers to write back to me on this especially economists The English language links Indians better than the national language, Hindi, especially as most parts of southern India still are The English language links Indians better than the national language, Hindi, especially as most parts of southern India still are not conversant in Hindi. Some parts of the southern part of India actually prefer English to Hindi for conversing with their northern Indian counterparts. This being the case, Sonia Gandhi's Hindi has been criticized, and in an official interview with the Congress leader, Priyanka Gandhi, Priyanka was quick to admit that Sonia Gandhi's Hindi was as good as her own and sometimes even words are quickly misinterpreted. This is an example of manipulated narrative

Sonia Gandhi had first-hand exposure to the world politics by direct observation when she lived under one roof, so to speak, with Indira Gandhi and Rajiv Gandhi. She never actively interfered in the politics or held any active political role during the reigns of Rajiv Gandhi; however, she observed everything that went on as perhaps a regular family affair. By the time Sonia Gandhi successfully took charge as president, she undoubtedly had nearly three persons' worth of exposure to politics, which surfaced clearly in her firm decisive role in a laudable informal and constructive way that simply appealed to the Congress party and the electorate alike.

Sonia Gandhi's Congress party welcomes any member who has faith in all appealing congress ideals of unity, tolerance, freedom, and democracy. Sonia Gandhi actively and dedicatedly hears all input from all levels of functioning within the Congress party as a responsible president. Perhaps she wishes to shoulder the responsibility of these congressional ideals. Most congress leaders are heard with earnestness in regular meetings that are well organized and led by Sonia Gandhi. Her noteworthy policies are those that were initiated by Rajiv Gandhi with special emphasis on less-empowered and economically less privileged classes of society like farmers and scheduled castes and tribes, for example. She is the only Indian woman politician who has had a set up special access to aggrieved women via the women grievance cell. Sonia Gandhi addresses issues concerning women via her team based in New Delhi. Her political decisions stem from a clear devotion to congress ideals; she is a silent crusader, ensuring the institution of the policies of Congress and always placing a much needed emphasis on the empowerment of women, and the interests of the farming community and communally disturbed communities. Soon after she was unanimously voted into the presidency of Congress party, she was unequivocally accepted, and her resignations during difficult situations have been turned down. Her strong leadership for nearly two decades has only strengthened the hopes of congressmen and congresswomen. Why then should there be a question of her maiden nationality in the global world that we live in today? Values must be accepted. We must not question gender, nationality, language, and other differences. Dear readers, I welcome you all to respect this question. Perhaps it is time we prevent 'the contorted and destructive force of hatred or discrimination' For if hatred and discrimination breed, the result is simply self-destruction of society and humanity. The only way out seems to be to adopt whatever prevents such thoughts of hatred or discrimination.

Globally it is easy to see that there is not a single place free from such discrimination. With *massive* globalisation, the world has become smaller than ever before. A single click of the mouse on the computer – even, better a simple tap on a touch screen – opens up global business and global life. Should we let discrimination and hatred ruin the unification of the world? Should we let the hatred or discrimination tear apart the world? Indeed, the choice is ours. We are creating war in every street of the world if we let hatred and discrimination flourish. We have the potential to destroy ourselves and the world eventually.

Why can't we, the so-called clever social human beings, work for a better world? We must invest the necessary time to work on not discriminating. We must work on something constructive and *stop* any form of hatred, bullying, and discrimination. Discrimination and hatred are worthless and nothing else. It is unbelievable that such forms of discrimination are televised, sponsored, and nourished, even spread nationally and internationally across the globe! It is only amazing.

Dear readers, I welcome each of you to reflect on this and actively discourage these needless traits of discrimination and hatred.

Instead, promote unity, tolerance, and freedom. It should start at your doorstep before it reaches the street and envelops and destroys the rest of the world in the form of wars, killings, attacks … the list seems simply endless. Just sit back and imagine what this world would have been like had there simply been no hatred, no discrimination, no wars, no racial attacks! Such a good feeling. Just imagining it gives such a relief. Imagine if we could work this out. We indeed can; it is easy and productive to cultivate moral values and enjoy them.

This can happen. When every human being pledges not to engage in discrimination or hatred, the world will surely be a much more lovable place to live in – our own world, for us together. In this direction

I feel privileged education(especially STEM for women) must be made free tax free and hugely funded more than defence spending more than war spending I feel education and retraining must be imposed instead of penalties and illegal treatment of unlawful global citizens Harvards should open up one branch in every nation and develop a public private partnership and enhance dissemination of true good knowledge and unity peace and freedom and prosperity High levels of education must bring out nonwar strategies to develop the world The whole world must engage in the safety and security of the whole world as first and second world war histories teach us no one is insulated from war tragedies Here is my dream proposition Harvards and similar world's best companies and people 'S constructive success stories should be universally promoted grown and nurtured world councils and agreements should be made to protect farmers,small and medium businesses,less priveleged women and children populations of the world,Hollywood should open up studios across the world and manage better success than current ones limiting markets only to the English speaking countries Media studies and Real estate should become bigger subjects and topics accessible for common men across the world. Countries shining in excellence in outputs like Japan models should be replicated across the world Movies,enetrtainment and all industries must do cross over across the world there is more output for the world There would then be no need to invent tariff at all forget reciprocal tariff Countries with untapped rich natural African resources must be opened up with negotiation and trade Globalisation must be facilitated rather curbing

More education is needed for cinema professionals,real estate professionals,media professionals and educationists in the near future These fields need more Research and developments Legislations worldwide must be amended in accordance with current provision practice and redistribution care housing and united nations human development indices must be adhered to strongly

By virtue of Sonia Gandhi's formalized wedding with Shri Rajiv Gandhi, her Indian citizenship is unequivocally clear. According to the Citizenship Act of 1955, women who are married to citizens of India become naturalized citizens. Yet time and again, while policies and matters of national and international interest spark conversations, Sonia Gandhi's foreign origin is ridiculed needlessly. To me, this is appalling indeed. I sincerely plead against such discrimination against Sonia Gandhi. It must stop. I strongly oppose such forces of hatred based on nationality, race, religion, or gender. I wonder if these needless, baseless controversies against Sonia Gandhi have affected the faith of the electorate in the Congress; it certainly could have affected the defeat of congressional ideals in the 2014 general elections.

One of the references quotes a Congress leader saying this about Sonia Gandhi: 'Sonia Gandhi is really the best man we got.' This describes the power of hard-work and strong leadership in Sonia Gandhi. Sonia Gandhi's real power is her acceptability as a leader by the congressmen. The Indian National Congress is the world's largest democratic party. The Congress is the time-tested party in India, as it is the only party that has successfully road tested many of its own policies and regulations, which have stood India in good stead. At the time Sonia Gandhi accepted the presidency of Congress in 1998, the Congress was not faring as well; it grossly lacked a strong leader. Sonia Gandhi, after accepting the presidency of the Indian National Congress, travelled a record 63,000 kilometres and made public speeches in at least sixty large public gatherings. These statistics are applicable only on the face of Congress's success in 2004.

There has been a record of her continuing public presences in her own constituency, Rae Bareli, and elsewhere in India when Congress needed a bolstered campaign across the country.

Sonia Gandhi is the most popular Gandhi in the world today.

After Sonia Gandhi became president of Indian National Congress, the faith in Congress got better, and the Congress party assumed power in fifteen states within just six years.

Sonia Gandhi edited two books, *Freedom's Daughter: Letters between Indira Gandhi and Jawaharlal Nehru: 1922–1939* and *Two Alone Two Together: Letters Between Indira Gandhi and Jawaharlal Nehru 1922–1964*, both published by Hodder & Stoughton with copyrights reserved to Priyanka Gandhi, congressional leader and daughter of Sonia Gandhi. She also has been awarded the Belgian honour of Grand Officer of the Order of Leopold. It was presented to her by Belgian Prime Minister Guy Verhofstadt. She was also given an honorary degree by the Free University of Brussels. Sonia Gandhi remarked clearly, 'One's real education is in the university of Life.'

This perhaps is relevant to Sonia Gandhi's own enriched accomplished life and career bringing values to the society she has lived in. Sonia Gandhi harnessed a potential think tank within the Congress, including the illustrious Dr Manmohan Singh, Pranab Mukherjee, Ahmed Patel, Dig Vijay Singh, Ashok Gehlot, and Ghulam Nabi Azad to name a few. Sonia Gandhi's support of Prathibha Patil was a milestone in making a woman president in India who successfully completed a term in Indian democracy. Sonia Gandhi's association with the illustrious Dr Manmohan Singh established her visionary abilities on dealing with many issues. One of the references quotes, My unequivocal view about Sonia Gandhi's achievements are that 'All the successes of the Congress under her undoubted leadership and powerful decisions 'have usefully resulted in the substantial success that Sonia Gandhi worked hard for that Congress ideals enjoyed ... Where there has been uninvited failures within the Congress and outside it has been largely because of nonacceptance of Congress ideology and lack of faith amongst people.

The recent elections in 2014 saw a massive failure in Congress, mainly because of a lack of effective marketing of congressional ideals, along with the fact that the electorate did not recognize the massive success of Sonia Gandhi's support of the UPA, which encourages the particular ideals of communal harmony, unity, and tolerance along with the uplifting of less-empowered sections in the society that no other party has singularly supported historically. Contrarily provocative speeches of hatred and discrimination won attention and even instigated the hitherto dormant youthful electorate of India, and this is what provided an opportunity for such a change. This is my view, and this expected change is yet to happen.

Sonia Gandhi is an exception to the dynastic rulers in the Gandhi family in that she executes enormous dynamism in contemporary politics in India. This perhaps was made possible because Sonia Gandhi hailed from a commoner's background and observed the efficacy and failures of decisions in politics by both Indira Gandhi and Rajiv Gandhi as a direct witness in the family. This is evident in evolving Congress policies apart from strengthening the previously successful policies by Rajiv Gandhi's government.

A reference from one of the books states, 'A decisive win would also entrench Sonia Gandhi as the party's leader as a foreign-born individual who is where she is because she married into the Gandhi dynasty.' I place my argument against this statement. This is a grossly discriminatory statement against Sonia Gandhi.

My unequivocal view is that Sonia Gandhi's achievements are the result of a clear, informed decision that she has made to help the Congress party and thereby help the electorate benefit from the ideals that the dynastic Gandhi family has fought for. Sonia Gandhi clearly did this without running in the race for the office of prime minister. She made a clear decision that baffled political critics across the world. She declined the office of prime minister in an official Congress meeting despite the huge pressure from congressmen who pleaded with her to accept and lead them successfully in governance. This is a classic example of her clearly grounded goals. She is not in a simple race for power.

There are many examples of politicians across the world who have stepped into dynastic ruling positions as heirs and failed miserably. Here is one of my favourite Sonia Gandhi quotes: 'I believe anger and hatred blind us.'

According to statistics reported by CNN in 2004, half of the Indian population was living on less than two dollars a day. Congress is the major party supporting rural Indian population.

On the duty of a politician, Sonia Gandhi wrote:

> I believe that while remaining representative of all interests, politics has a particular duty to those in need. As a politician in a country where many still live in poverty, it is my obligation and my responsibility to strive to empower the poor and the vulnerable. At times, this means being willing to fight entrenched social injustice. Indeed, the Indian, so long disempowered by poverty, has a greater claim on the fruits of our growing prosperity. To eradicate poverty, inequality and injustice from our society is an enormous task and it does remain our motivating goal. There are some who argue that faster growth will in the long run solve problems of social inequality and poverty and narrow the gap between rich and the poor. My aim in politics has always been to do whatever I can in my own way to defend the secular, democratic foundations of our country and to address the concerns and aspirations of the many whose voice often remains unheard.

Sonia Gandhi advocated austerity for all the congress MPs and set an example by travelling in economy class on her 14 September 2009 travel from New Delhi to Mumbai. She saved Rs 10,000. She also advocated for contribution of 20 per cent of MPs salary for the drought affected victims in India.

Sonia Gandhi said in one of her speeches: 'The Congress is unique. Our uniqueness arises from several basic features of the Congress history, its character, its ideology and the legacy of its leadership. I am convinced that the time is ripe for a massive renaissance of our political culture so that we build that society which combines compassion with competence, equity with excellence.'

As Mani Shankar Aiyer of the CP told Bill Schneider of CNN. com, 'She is the queen. She is appointing a regent to run some of the business of government for her. But it is she who will be in charge and who will continue to direct the fortunes of the Congress Party.' Sonia Gandhi has held the following positions:

- President, Indian National Congress (March 1998 onwards)
- Chairperson, Congress (I) Parliamentary Party (CPP)
- Elected to 13th Lok Sabha (1999)
- Leader of Opposition, Lok Sabha
- Member, General Purposes Committee (1999–2000)
- Re-elected to 14th Lok Sabha (second term) (2004)
- Chairperson, United Progressive Alliance
- Chairperson, National Advisory Council (2004–22 March 2006)
- Resigned from 14th Lok Sabha (23 March 2006)
- Re-elected in a bye-election (15 May 2006)
- Re-elected to 15th Lok Sabha (3rd term) (2009)

Other affiliations:

- Chairperson of Rajiv Gandhi Foundation, Indira Gandhi Memorial Trust and Jawaharlal Nehru Memorial Fund
- President of Swaraj Bhavan Trust and Kamla Nehru Memorial Hospital Society
- Trustee of Jalianwala Bagh National Memorial Trust
- Member of Nehru Memorial Museum and Library

Sonia Gandhi also is the eighth person of foreign origin to be the president of the Indian National Congress.

Sonia Gandhi wrote, 'I came to relish the flavours of India's many cuisines, to feel comfortable in Indian clothes, to speak Hindi and acquaint myself with the cultural heritage of my new homeland.

The glorious and multi-hued palette of India came to be as dear and precious to me as it was to them [Indira Gandhi and Rajiv Gandhi].' These words from Sonia Gandhi clearly highlight her passion for and love of India.

Sonia Gandhi brought in the assets of modifying, re-invigorating, and adapting the Congress party through her innovations in the party as president. Her presidency has been unopposed consistently by an overwhelming majority, and her resignations declined by the same overwhelming majority of party men in the Congress party.

But with her throngs of supporters, some travelling far distances from neighbouring villages just to have a glimpse of her, Sonia has shown that she has no need for top offices. She was the inspiration behind two of the Congress-led government's most important policies concerning rural jobs. She supported an joint initiative between the United Progressive Alliance (UPA) and Congress that brought in enormous funds that were allocated to the rural population, which is the majority in India. She supported regulation of policies to the middle class while diverting funds to the starving rural population. Any other party may barely understand such an initiative let alone execute it.

Sonia Gandhi excels at spearheading such needed policies to success. Many of the policies pioneered by the UPA are the result of Sonia Gandhi's much-needed input as she works for the Congress party's manifestos. No other party can achieve the success of policies like the policies initiated by the Sonia Gandhi–supported UPA. She also backed a program related to the priority use of land for economic development in a discretionary manner. No other party other than the Congress party could pioneer such policies let alone maintain them.

Sonia Gandhi said, in December 2013, that her party had not 'been able to convince the people of our policies, programmes and achievements'.

The Congress party has won and lost many elections. In victory or defeat, we must remember that it is our solemn duty to serve people to the best of our ability.'

Sonia Gandhi no doubt also watched and learned as Indira Gandhi fought a variety of political battles.

Sonia Gandhi's popularity is evidence that nations can overcome prejudices of gender roles, religion, and ethnicity in leadership when the person in that position pursues the good of that nation over his or her own political ambition.

Facts we have learned from Sonia Gandhi's interviews on national television:

- Both she and her husband were initially disinclined to enter politics.
- The reason she entered politics about seven years after an initial refusal was to strengthen Congress.
- Sonia Gandhi clarifies how she understood why her husband's supporters in politics left the party, and she clearly remains non-judgemental about it aptly and fairly. One can infer this clearly as she is neither critical nor cynical about it.
- Sonia Gandhi has given natural, widely publicized interviews apart from her regular campaigning speeches across the subcontinent.
- Sonia Gandhi also has publicly, in an interview, welcomed the passage of the Women's Reservation Bill in the Parliament.

- She is articulate and comfortable while communicating in Hindi, the national language of India.
- Sonia Gandhi also mentions her father's clear disapproval of her marriage to Shri Rajiv Gandhi. She mentioned he tried to persuade her by giving her a train ticket to return from Hindustan back to Italy. She hadn't thought about this for a long time, as her decision to become Indian had become foremost in her life. She was clear that her father seemed to come to terms with this later on. She was also clear to say that her father's opposition was mainly because he didn't want her to permanently move to a foreign country, which she would if he approved her marriage. He was also understandably concerned about the safety of his daughter.
- Remarkably, the one time her face brightened up was when she was mentioning her relationship with her mother-in-law, Indira Gandhi. Her face shone when she reminisced about the former prime minister.
- Sonia Gandhi also was clear about the fact that she was not power hungry; she spoke with effortless and spontaneous eloquence.
- She stated that her decades of presidency in Congress are testimony to these facts.
- Sonia Gandhi clarified that she makes all political decisions independently while acting as a president in the Congress and yet gets all information from within the party. (This clearly contradicts a widely publicized rumour that Sonia Gandhi does not interfere in the day-to-day functioning of the government and that she lacks the ability to do so.)
- Sonia Gandhi also stated clearly that she initially opposed Rajiv's move into politics as she was scared he would meet the same fate her mother-in-law, Indira Gandhi, suffered. She is

articulate and comfortable while communicating in Hindi, the national language of India.

- Sonia Gandhi also mentions her father's clear disapproval of her marriage to Shri Rajiv Gandhi. She mentioned he tried to persuade her by giving her a train ticket to return from Hindustan back to Italy. She hadn't thought about this for a long time, as her decision to become Indian had become foremost in her life. She was clear that her father seemed to come to terms with this later on. She was also clear to say that her father's opposition was mainly because he didn't want her to permanently move to a foreign country, which she would if he approved her marriage. He was also understandably concerned about the safety of his daughter.

- Remarkably, the one time her face brightened up was when she was mentioning her relationship with her mother-in-law, Indira Gandhi. Her face shone when she reminisced about the former prime minister.

- Sonia Gandhi also was clear about the fact that she was not power hungry; she spoke with effortless and spontaneous eloquence.

- She stated that her decades of presidency in Congress are testimony to these facts.

- Sonia Gandhi clarified that she makes all political decisions independently while acting as a president in the Congress and yet gets all information from within the party. (This clearly contradicts a widely publicized rumour that Sonia Gandhi does not interfere in the day-to-day functioning of the government and that she lacks the ability to do so.)

- Sonia Gandhi also stated clearly that she initially opposed Rajiv's move into politics as she was scared he would meet the same fate her mother-in-law, Indira Gandhi, suffered.

While in current contemporary politics it is the norm to publicize manifestos, debate about probable legislations, and rake in unnecessary controversies, Sonia Gandhi has played unconventional uniquely successful politics in that she has proven to be more of an executive politician than an oratory politician. She has always been focused on commenting on only matters that are relevant.

Sonia Gandhi has chosen carefully premeditated public statements which many congressman follow as part of party's discipline. Indeed she is the leader in this.

I was dismayed at some speculation in the public domain that mentions her failings. I see most of them as stages of evolution. She is a clever leader with a natural skill and understanding to remain optimistic about the future, especially the political future of the Congress party.

Quotes by and about Sonia Gandhi:

The Congress is the only party that can provide peace and stability to the state.

The lifestyle of many of our colleagues has been very pompous. They conduct weddings and birthdays in such an ostentatious manner that it pains me a lot. It appears that they are making fun of our commitment to the poor.

Together we can face any challenges as deep as the ocean and as high as the sky.

Sonia is a very private person, yet she is enigmatic. I wrote this book in 2003 when Sonia's political rating was low, but I knew she would turn around the Congress political future. She is an ordinary person with extra ordinary qualities.

The future for each of us is interconnected, and all of us should work together by following the path laid down by former leaders of the party for the development of the country and its brighter future.

Sonia Gandhi continued to be part of The National Advisory Council (NAC) of India and held two public offices. She was asked to resign from one of the offices, but I have reason to believe that this should not be seen as a failure. It indeed speaks volumes of her commitment and ability to take on the stress and resilience of the ever-metamorphosing politics.

It is noteworthy that she upholds the integrity of congress for it and whilst there is a national and international debate about polarising politics. I have reason to believe that only emphasizes Sonia Gandhi's ability to lead; it is the most important ingredient with which to infuse the essence of leadership. I see that in Sonia Gandhi; she is the epitome of an archetypical leader.

The dignity and respect she has displayed are an inspirational story for the silent winner. What began as a simple love affair in the 1960s with the charming Rajiv Gandhi brought her into a path of responsibility as a single mother, a widow, a mother-in-law, and a grandmother. The successive victories she gained in the elections are testimony to the acceptance of her political leadership and the faith and trust the electorate has placed in her. This is not just the vote for 'Gandhi'; it is the vote for this woman who stood strong and unshakeable. She concentrated on her faith and determination to lead the Congress party, and her dedication superseded the many divisive and disturbing forces that worked to oust her and the Congress party.

She has earned the respect she now receives. She looks up to her long-lasting faith and love for her late husband, Rajiv Gandhi, and her

The future for each of us is interconnected, and all of us should work together by following the path laid down by former leaders of the party for the development of the country and its brighter future.

Sonia Gandhi continued to be part of The National Advisory Council (NAC) of India and held two public offices. She was asked to resign from one of the offices, but I have reason to believe that this should not be seen as a failure. It indeed speaks volumes of her commitment and ability to take on the stress and resilience of the ever-metamorphosing politics.

It is noteworthy that she upholds the integrity of congress for it and whilst there is a national and international debate about polarising politics. I have reason to believe that only emphasizes Sonia Gandhi's ability to lead; it is the most important ingredient with which to infuse the essence of leadership. I see that in Sonia Gandhi; she is the epitome of an archetypical leader.

The dignity and respect she has displayed are an inspirational story for the silent winner. What began as a simple love affair in the 1960s with the charming Rajiv Gandhi brought her into a path of responsibility as a single mother, a widow, a mother-in-law, and a grandmother. The successive victories she gained in the elections are testimony to the acceptance of her political leadership and the faith and trust the electorate has placed in her. This is not just the vote for 'Gandhi'; it is the vote for this woman who stood strong and unshakeable. She concentrated on her faith and determination to lead the Congress party, and her dedication superseded the many divisive and disturbing forces that worked to oust her and the Congress party.

She has earned the respect she now receives. She looks up to her long-lasting faith and love for her late husband, Rajiv Gandhi, and her late mother-in-law, Indira Gandhi. This is truly a unique *saas-bahu* story – daughter-in-law and mother-in-law story – that is very rare in contemporary times.

Sonia Gandhi's political success is the result of many qualities:

- Carefully premeditated interviews and speeches
- Hard work and determination to avoid being bated by opposing forces
- A keen sense of responsibility
- Great focus
- Lack of emotional behaviour in leadership
- Rich experience gained by passive observation while living under the same roof with three generations of successful and important politicians
- Remarkable decision-making skills when supporting powerful congressional think tank members such as P. Chidambaram and Pranab Mukherjee
- Ability to single-handedly shoulder the responsibility of the Congress party and her family responsibility
- Growing enthusiasm to increase hope for the believers in Congress by promoting foundations under her husband's name and renewing other similar social organisations named after the illustrious Gandhi family
- Commitment and duty to maintain her love and commitment to the family by working for the same ideals that the family sacrificed for Sonia Gandhi certainly deserves a great deal of respect, for she has toiled hard to let the Congress tree grow into the entity it is today.

Sonia Gandhi has passionately worked for the policies that have been landmarks in India's political history. No other politician in he current times has evoked such a sense of duty and persistence in serving the cause of the 2014 motto of the Congress party: *Har Hath Shakti, Har Hath Tarakki* (power in every hand, progress to everyone). The results of such a duty have been so evident in her actions, such as deciding to decline the office of prime minister, the highest post that beckoned her. Often those who serve as Congress president actively seek the post of prime minister.

She is a great politician because she clearly has worked hard for the policies the Congress collectively worked for. She worked behind the scenes, so to speak, and successfully strengthened the position of Congress despite relinquishing the highest office of the prime minister.

The reason for the resounding success of Congress in 2004 is the hard work and responsibility of Sonia Gandhi to help people appreciate the ideals of the Congress. There was huge unrest amongst party congressmen that Sonia Gandhi should become the prime minister. What is absolutely clear is that her decision not to become the prime minister was a firm, personal, political decision in keeping with the plan to serve the party. She made that decision in clarity and with resolution. She always officially declared that she never was after the position, and she quite clearly lived up to this statement during her entire tenure. It is a legendary decision, and many stories have circulated that attempt to explain it, but they remain speculations only. Sonia Gandhi perhaps realized she would have found it difficult to perform in any other capacity than Congress president. She also, it appears, was aware that perhaps running the race for the position would diminish her ability to uphold her job of shaping Congress. With this in mind Sonia Gandhi chaired the National Advisory Council, which drew criticism – a criticism, I believe, that has no cognisable basis.

Sonia Gandhi wipes back her tears of remembrance for her dear husband, Shri Rajiv Gandhi. The future political promise, Rahul

Gandhi, their son, looks on, perhaps feeling the tears of pain his mother sheds. Heartfelt moments for the Gandhi Family! Sonia Gandhi wipes a tear at 13th death anniversary of her dear husband Rajiv Gandhi at Bir Bhoomi New Delhi on May 21 2004. Rajiv Gandhi was allegedly murdered on May 21 1991 by Srilankan seperatists in Sriperumbudur near Madras.

However, Sonia Gandhi was forced to quit the position of chair of the National Advisory Council, which simply appeared as a move to destabilise the Congress presidency and its influence on the United Progressive Alliance. Some authorities viewed this as a setback for Sonia Gandhi, but my simple view is that any alliance or Congress is simply nonexistent without Sonia Gandhi. S is simply nonexistent without Sonia Gandhi. Sonia Gandhi reserves the right to function as her responsibility permits her to, and if this meant chairing the National Advisory Council, it should not have been questioned in the first instance.

The Congress party and its functions in India stand firm today on the foundation strengthened by Sonia Gandhi. And so it is right and correct, in governing the situation, to influence the UPA through the National Advisory Council or the Congress Party or perhaps the decisions emerging out of Sonia Gandhi herself. This indeed is the political success of sorts as those would then have been the chosen avenues for the Congress to implement its policies or manifestos or achieve governance.

The Congress party is the longest-serving party in Indian history.

It has been the time-tested party since India gained independence in 1947. The party road tested many pioneering policies that would not have been easily stabilized by any other party. Sonia Gandhi is the sixth successor in the Nehru-Gandhi family, the others being Motilal Nehru, Jawaharlal Nehru, and Indira Gandhi.

Indira Gandhi, Sanjay Gandhi, Rajiv Gandhi, and Sonia Gandhi have been the frontline of politics for many years. They are the first family of India.

Sonia Gandhi was elected successfully first from Amethi Lok Sabha, the constituency that Rajiv Gandhi held, and was also elected successfully from Bellary Lok Sabha constituency. (Lok Sabha is the lower house in the Indian Parliament.) She later won in the Rae Bareli Lok Sabha constituency in the Uttar Pradesh state.

Sonia Gandhi is a member of Parliament and represents the Rae Bareli constituency. This is a separate position from her post as president of the Congress party. In a press release in 2015, Sonia Gandhi expressed an intention to hand over her responsibility for the Rae Bareli constituency to its elected deputy vice president, Rahul Gandhi, her son.

Priyanka Gandhi, the ever-attractive daughter of Sonia Gandhi and Rajiv Gandhi, is a Congress party leader. She enjoys enormous popularity and is a powerful leader by nature, no doubt. I believe she will add dynamic dimensions to Congress. She is a politician to watch in the years to come. Despite immense pressure, Priyanka Gandhi played a secondary role in the family in serving the Congress party, as per the decisions of her mother and the congress president, Sonia Gandhi. Sonia Gandhi has nourished a powerful congress leader in Priyanka Gandhi, in a significantly timely manner.Now Priyanka Gandhi elevates to the frontgate with effortless exponential ablity to lead Congress

The growing expectations of the estimated 300 million Indian youth involve the following:

- They have increased expectations of government.
- Indian youth and first-time voters were swayed to the 'media hype' of what they could expect from a government other than the Congress.

- The Indian National Congress's youth wing has not adequately marketed its policies.

No matter what, an amount of indifference may exist because of discrimination against Sonia Gandhi's work in Congress. I believe, however, that she has achieved peerless political excellence. I plead with every democrat to stop discrimination on the basis of gender, nationality, language, or culture. Instead, embrace the marvellous and excellent political job she has done in politics as president of Congress. It is time Sonia Gandhi is given due recognition and acceptance, and I invite every reader to reflect on what could be done to spread the principal message of unity, tolerance, and freedom as well as non-violence and non-discrimination over many divergent characteristics. I plead with all readers to welcome the universal values of tolerance, unity, and freedom by shunning discrimination and hatred based on nationality, gender, language, culture, and any others on a long list of characteristics.

If the Congress party welcomes this, I am certain every human being should agree. I urge you to welcome a new whole world of *love*, *tolerance*, *unity*, and *freedom*. It is in your hands as much as it is in mine, and thereby it is in the hands of everyone in the whole world.

Please think about this. I welcome you to respect Sonia Gandhi for her ideals and her faith in the Congress. And at least consider this rather than breeding hatred or discrimination because she is a foreign-born individual or a woman or a widow or that she may not be fluent in an Indian language. Sonia Gandhi's dedication to her work and to the ideals of Congress should overpower any such discriminatory characteristics and the many policies of Congress that have increased India's global presence in the economic world.

I have enjoyed the process of re-discovering the long-forgotten magic in Sonia Gandhi that moulded today's Congress by dedicating this book to Sonia Gandhi's congressional ideals, and I hope each reader will give earnest thought to my numerously repeated messages of unity, tolerance, and freedom. If a significant number of readers can achieve this, I take this opportunity to thank you. Then my book will have served its purpose of spreading this strong message. This will heal a world that is suffering, and it will inspire the creation of a better world of peace.

What is the future of the Congress presidency? Sonia Gandhi, it is apparent, has worked to unify the Congress party across the subcontinent by dint of hard work, determination, and dedication. It would be easy for us to conclude that her presidency may be handed over to any congressman or congresswoman as it happens Mallikarjun Kharge leads as a President. In a recent official press release, it was announced that Sonia Gandhi's tenure as president of Congress has been extended, with a plan for her to leave the post to any other successor she chooses. With her decisions in the past always made to uphold the ideals of Congress, I am certain her decision will not be one to protect any unilateral self- interests.

Current positions are varied different and unexpected for any Congress person and all three members Sonia Gandhi,Priyanka Gandhi and Rahul Gandhi now function in the Indian politics with robust vigor and am certain politics can be hoped to get better As my book has not been officially endorsed by either the Indian National Congress or any congressman or congresswoman, including Sonia Gandhi, I have had no access to detailed policies and regulations that have positively promoted India's economic development. I certainly would take any such opportunity to elaborate such details in any future parts of this series. All my thoughts about varied policies of the

Congress that I mention in this book stem from my own membership of the Indian electorate for a significant period of at least a decade..

Sonia Gandhi's support for a rather difficult alliance has won the Bihar legislative assembly election, in November 2015. She led many useful campaigns to encourage and acknowledge the support. The Bihar win is a testimony of how faith in the Congress is being restored.

Thank you for reading this book. I hope take away a strong message of peace, harmony, and freedom – attributes that can help ram certain her decision will not be one to protect any self-interests. Current positions are varied different and unexpected for any Congress person and all three members Sonia Gandhi,Priyanka Gandhi and Rajiv Gandhi now function in the Indian politics with robust vigor and am certain politics can be hoped to get better

As my book has not been officially endorsed by either the Indian National Congress or any congressman or congresswoman, including Sonia Gandhi, I have had no access to detailed policies and regulations that have positively promoted India's economic development. I certainly would take any such opportunity to elaborate such details in any future parts of this series. All my thoughts about varied policies of the Congress that I mention in this book stem from my own membership of the Indian electorate for a significant period of at least a decade.. I do hope I will get such an opportunity., I do hope i may touch upon such matters earnestly to increase the deserving image of the political ideals of Sonia Gandhi that have maintained India in good stead on an international platform.

Sonia Gandhi's support for a rather difficult alliance has won the Bihar legislative assembly election, in November 2015. She led many useful campaigns to encourage and acknowledge the support. The Bihar win is a testimony of how faith in the Congress is being restored.

Thank you for reading this book. I hope take away a strong message of peace, harmony, and freedom – attributes that can help the world to develop and progress and become a beautiful world that is a better place to live. I like to share the feedback of a reader from New Zealand who found reading this book 'intellectually frustrating'

I welcome you to read my future editions of this book series.

REFERENCES

Ansari, Yusuf (Yusuf Ahmad), *Triumph of will, Sonia Gandhi* (New Delhi: Tara-India Research Press, 2006).

Bakshi, S. R. and S. R. Sharma, S. Gajrani, eds., *Sonia Gandhi, the President of AICC* (New Delhi: APH Pub. Corp, 1998).

Bhanot, Arun, Suraj Prasad Verma, Mahesh Sharma, Arun Bhanot, *Sonia Gandhi: A Biography* (New Delhi: Diamond, 2004).

Caudharī, Sūryanārāyaṇa, *Soniyā Gāṅdhī: sattā saṅgharsha* (Jayapura: Bāla Mandira, 2000).

Chatterjee, Rupa, *Sonia Gandhi: the Lady in Shadow* (Delhi: Butala, 1998).

Chatterjee, Rupa, *The Sonia Mystique* (New Delhi: Virgo Publications, 2000).

Dehlavi, Ishtiaq Ahmad, ed, *Bhārat ratan Indirā Gāndhī se Soniyā Gandhī tak = Bharat ratan Indira Gandhi to Sonia Gandhi / murattabah, Ishtiyāq Aḥmad Dihlavī* (Dehli: Maktabah-yi Zauq-i Salīm, 2004).

Deshpande, A., 'Sonia Gandhi's Nationality: Politics and Xenophobia', *Economic and Political Weekly*, 34/21 (1999), 1241–1242.

Gandhi, Rajiv, *Rajiv's World: Photographs by Rajiv Gandhi; Introduction by Sonia Gandhi* (New Delhi: Viking; London: Penguin, 1994).

Gandhi, Sonia, ed., *Freedom's Daughter: Letters between Indira Gandhi and Jawaharlal Nehru: 1922–1939* (London: Hodder & Stoughton, 1988).

Gandhi, Sonia, ed., *Two Alone Two Together: Letters Between Indira Gandhi and Jawaharlal Nehru 1922–1964* (London: Hodder & Stoughton, 2004).

Ganesan, P. C., Sonia Gandhi: the Unfolding Scenario (Chennai: Sura, 2002).

Gupta, Ramesh, *Sonia in Command* (Delhi: Indian Publishers' Distributors, 2005).

Jai, Janak and Rajiv Jai, *Sonia's Foreign Origin: A Non-Issue* (New Delhi: Regency Publications, c2004).

Kamala, Ema, *Soniyā Gāndhī: utkarsha se nepathya taka* (Dillī: Sneha Sāhitya Sadana, 2004).

Khaṇḍela, Māna Canda, *Soniyā Gāṅdhī aura Bhāratīya rājanīti* (Jayapura: Poinṭara Pabliśarsa, 2005).

Khare, H., 'Collected Words of Sonia Gandhi', *Seminar*, 480 (1999), 61-65.

Kidwai, Rasheed, *Sonia: A Biography* (New Delhi ; London: Penguin/ Viking, 2003).

Kumāra, Avadheśa, Soniyā Gāndhī, Kāṅgresa, evaṃ vartamāna rājanīti (Dillī: Ākṛti Prakāśana, 2008).

McGowan, J., 'Sonia Gandhi Steps Down', *Commonweal*, 131/12 (2004), 8-9.

Mishra, Shubha Raj and Yashpal Singh Chauhan, *Sonia Gandhi: saga of service* (New Delhi: Shabd Prakashan, 1998).

Phaḍake, Ya. Di., *Bhāratīya nāgarikatva* (Mumbaī: Akshara Prakāśana, 2004).akash, A. Surya, ed., *Sonia Under Scrutiny: Issue of Foreign Origin* (New Delhi: India First Foundation, 2004).

Prakash, A Surya, ed., Sonia under Scrutiny: Issue of Foreign Origin (New Delhi: India First Foundation, 2004).

Sanghvi, Vijay, *The Congress: Indira to Sonia Gandhi* (Delhi: Kalpaz Publications, 2006.)

Sarkar, N. I., *Sonia Gandhi: Tryst with India* (New Delhi: Atlantic Publishers & Distributors, c2007).

Sarswat, Madhvanand and Nitin Kumar Mohanlal Bora, *Great lady of the world: Sonia Gandhi* (Pilani: Priyanka Prakashan, 2013).

Satpathy, Biswajit, *Sonia Gandhi: Return of the Red Rose* (New Delhi: Dominant Publishers and Distributors, c2005).

Sharma, Pranika, *Sonia Gandhi* (International Publishers India: New Delhi, 1997).

Singh, Darshan, *Sonia Gandhi: Tryst with Destiny* (New Delhi: United Children's Movement, 2004).

Singh, Rani (Rani Gagan Deep), Sonia Gandhi: An Extraordinary Life, An Indian Destiny (Basingstoke: Palgrave Macmillan, 2011).

'Sonia Gandhi: A Successful Decade', *The Economist*, 8572 (2008), 74.

'Sonia Gandhi Changes Her Mind', *The Economist*, 4 June (1999), 80.

'Sonia Gandhi's Easy Win', *The Economist*, 24 November (2000), 105.

'Sonia Gandhi's Election Role', *The Economist*, 6 February (1998), 73.

'Sonia Gandhi withdraws', *The Economist*, 28 May (1999), 90-92.

Sood, P., *Sonia Gandhi: Trails of Triumph* (New Delhi: Vitasta Pub., c2009).

Śrīśaraṇa, *Soniyā Gāndhi: saumya aura nishṭhāvāna nārī* / Śrī Śaraṇa, Āloka *Kumāra Rastogī* (Dillī: Prema Prakāśana Mandira, 2005).

Tripathi, Madhusoodan and Nishant Singh, *Sonia Gandhi: the Jewel of India* (New Delhi: Radha Publications, 2007).

Vajra, Purūshottama, *Soniyā eka: jīvanta gāthā* (Dillī: Racanā Pablikeśansa, 2006).

Varde, Ashwin and The Editors of Society, *Sonia: The Untold Story* (Mumbai: Magna Books, 2004).

hārat ratan Indirā Gāndhī se Soniyā Gandhī tak = Bharat ratan Indira Gandhi to Sonia Gandhi / murattabah, Ishtiyāq Aḥmad Dihlavī ; compiled by Ishtiaq Ahmad Dehlavi.

ABOUT THE BOOK

I take great pleasure in presenting my book, Sonia Gandhi: The Power, Part I, to curious readers and critics. I hope those who read my book will respect the power in what I love to believe is phenomenal in politics. I also hope that my book is a source of inspiration to many women like myself who struggle to live a challenging life abroad. Acceptance means so much to people who work abroad, and I have struggled to express my feelings. Simply put, if there is no acceptance of ideals, then they fail to flourish as they should do. I sincerely hope that, with globalization, people and their values be widely accepted regardless of religion, colour, creed, race, and nationality, for certainly there should be no discrimination on the basis of any of these characteristics.

It is sad to see many ideals and values being crushed because they do not represent a particular 'nation', a particular religion, a particular race, a particular language, a particular gender -- the list of characteristics seems to never end. Imagine one whole world of peace where discrimination has ceased. This may seem like a dream, but I believe it is possible, and I hope my readers feel the same way after reading this book.

Sonia Gandhi, I strongly feel, should be accepted for her strong determination to challenge the odds as she works for the larger good